D. L. Moody wrote: "If we live for G  kingdom of darkness and the kingdon the kingdom of darkness is permitted to *if you* want to be popular in heaven, and get a reward that shall last forever, you will have to be unpopular here." Moody Bible Institute has a history of training and equipping soldiers to enter into the kingdom of darkness and fight for the souls of man. In Marvin Newell's A Martyr's Grace, you will read about twenty-one Moody students who were found "unpopular" among militants, combatants, guerrillas, rebels, extremists, communists, and bandits, all because they chose to engage in the battle for souls in God's kingdom. After reading their stories of relentless courage and resolve in the face of death, you will be challenged and inspired to live a life engaged in the same battle and consider it an honor to fight alongside others who are "unpopular."

Tom White
Executive Director
The Voice of the Martyrs, USA

Missionaries have been described as ordinary people with an extraordinary calling. Dr. Newell's compelling research of these who were called to martyrdom is both inspiring and instructive. Each step of obedience these servants took brought them closer to God until one day—quite unexpectedly in most cases—they found themselves in His very presence. Our call into ministry is not without cost. Some in our churches today must answer the call to the hard places. I highly recommend this book as an excellent way to enrich our understanding of being called into missionary service. I am looking forward to the day when there will be no need for a martyr's grace, but until that day comes, these stories powerfully demonstrate God's faithfulness to those He called to martyrdom.

Dr. Mike McDowell
Mission Pastor
Christ Community Church—Zion, IL

Psalm 46:10 reads, in part: "Cease striving and know that I am God." A Martyr's Grace stops us in our tracks as we reflect on brothers and sisters in Christ who were called upon to give their all. Story after story draws the reader to consider afresh what God calls us to, and what we as leaders are calling others into. The lives detailed here resonate with the rest of Psalm 46:10: "I will be exalted among the nations, I will be exalted in all the earth." In the end, it is God who is calling and we don't know where that might lead. We do know that ultimately, it will end with Him.

Rev. Greg H. Parsons
General Director
USCWM

In Africa, I stood before hallowed soil at the grave markers of missionaries, some of whom had died violently for the cause of Christ. I was sobered and at the same time motivated in my own service to Christ. Dr. Newell's work serves as an important marker to remember and honor some of those who experienced A Martyr's Grace. This book is carefully researched with grace, and Dr. Newell in his telling of the stories has preserved the dignity of those who suffered under brutal hands. In their own words taken from their letters and journals, the missionaries' thoughts and motives ring clear. Loss for Christ is always gain.

Dr. John H. Orme
Executive Director
IFMA—Wheaton, IL 60189

This is a very unusual and challenging book. It will not be easy to read, especially in this day of so much shallow commitment to the Lord. These are people who truly gave their all and we can learn so much from them.

George Verwer
Operation Mobilization

In reading this book, I was struck again by how "ordinary" these martyrs were. Yes, many had outstanding abilities and displayed mature Christian character even during their school years, but, as the author points out, no one would have picked them out during their days at Moody as future martyrs.

Yet, as martyrs, most of the people Marvin Newell writes about had an incredible impact on the kingdom of God. The martyrdom of Arthur Tylee and Mildred Kratz was the event that most shaped South America (Indian) Mission for two decades after their death and still has an impact on us today.

Their story, along with that of the nineteen other "Moody Martyrs" will encourage you to entrust your life to God and allow Him to use you for His glory as He chooses.

BILL OGDEN
Executive Director
South America Mission

Will the 21st century witness many martyrs for Christ? Will North American Christians suffer persecution in great gospel advance? Signs point that way. Marv Newell's inspiring collection of Moody Bible Institute students who've suffered martyrs' deaths while on mission for Christ will provide wisdom for the future by looking to the past. Moody grads, missionaries, and all believers will be blessed to consider afresh the cost of the cross for 21st century faith.

JIM O'NEILL
President, CrossWorld

A MARTYR'S GRACE

21 MOODY BIBLE INSTITUTE ALUMNI WHO GAVE THEIR LIVES FOR CHRIST

MARVIN J. NEWELL

MOODY PUBLISHERS
CHICAGO

© 2006 by
MARVIN J. NEWELL

All rights reserved. No part of this book may be reproduced in any form without permission in writing from the publisher, except in the case of brief quotations embodied in critical articles or reviews.

All Scripture quotations, unless otherwise indicated, are taken from the *New American Standard Bible*®, © Copyright The Lockman Foundation 1960, 1962, 1963, 1968, 1971, 1972, 1973, 1975, 1977, 1995. Used by permission.

Scripture quotations marked NIV are taken from the *Holy Bible, New International Version*®. NIV®. Copyright © 1973, 1978, 1984 by International Bible Society. Used by permission of Zondervan Publishing House. All rights reserved.

Scripture quotations marked KJV are taken from the King James Version.

Cover Design: Erik M. Peterson
Illustrations: Andy McGuire
Editor: Pam Pugh

Library of Congress Cataloging-in-Publication Data

Newell, Marvin J.
    A martyr's grace : 21 Moody Bible Institute alumni who gave their lives for Christ / by Marvin J. Newell.
        p. cm.
    Includes bibliographical references.
    ISBN-13: 978-0-8024-1448-9
    1. Christian martyrs. 2. Moody Bible Institute—Students. 3. Christian biography. I. Title.

BR1601.3.N49 2006
272'.9—dc22

                                                                2006016787

We hope you enjoy this book from Moody Publishers. Our goal is to provide high-quality, thought-provoking books and products that connect truth to your real needs and challenges. For more information on other books and products written and produced from a biblical perspective, go to www.moodypublishers.com or write to:

Moody Publishers
820 N. LaSalle Boulevard
Chicago, IL 60610

1 3 5 7 9 10 8 6 4 2

Printed in the United States of America

Contents

Foreword

When a school's history spans 130 years, it gains many treasures. God has lavishly blessed The Moody Bible Institute, where I have the privilege of serving as president. Among our treasures are a legacy of faithfulness to God and His Word, a swath of outstanding professors, and faithful, kingdom-building alumni spanning the globe. "God bless the school that D. L. Moody founded" rings the first line of our school's anthem, and it seems God has been answering that prayer for quite some time.

Upon reading this book, however, I see we are at risk of forgetting one of our greatest treasures: the memory of our martyrs. These are students who once walked our hallowed halls in preparation for Christ's service, and sometime later walked bravely into danger for His sake. They each made the ultimate sacrifice, giving their lives in service to the Master. A forgotten treasure is not a cherished one, and the memory of these martyrs is too precious to let fade, especially since they were of our fold.

For this reason, I heartily commend *A Martyr's Grace* to you. It tells the story of each of the twenty-one Moody Bible Institute alumni who gave their lives for Christ, the first in 1898, the last in 2002. In reading these stories, you will be moved to treasure not only their sacrifice, but also the deposit entrusted to you: the gospel of our Lord.

The names of these twenty-one are listed on a board in the foyer of Moody's Torrey-Gray auditorium, marked by asterisks to signal martyrdom. Our students walk by this board almost every day, most of them unaware of the price their forerunners paid. They are also unaware of what the future holds for them, and if they also will meet a martyr's end. No one knows. But we can all pray, "Lord, if the time comes, grant me a martyr's grace."

Here are twenty-one to whom it was granted.

J. PAUL NYQUIST, PhD
President
The Moody Bible Institute

"Have you grace to be a martyr?"

"Have you grace to be a martyr?" D. L. Moody was once asked.

"No," he replied, "I have not. But if God wanted me to be one, He would give me a martyr's grace."[1]

A martyr's grace is a special gift granted to a select few. Of the thousands of graduates of the Moody Bible Institute who have entered Christian service, less than two dozen have been granted this grace. Whereas scores of graduates have died while doing ministry, only a few have died a "martyr's death."

Many of these deaths were remembered for a time but have since been forgotten. Some of these stories have remained untold altogether until now. A few are rather familiar, and one or two continue to be renowned. However, all of these martyrs had death experiences that are compelling and worthy of remembrance.

The twenty-one martyrs in this book had very little in common. Only three threads seemingly tie them together: all had studied at the Moody Bible Institute, all were serving as missionaries when their lives were taken, and all have been officially declared martyrs by the school.

While they were students in training at Moody, none of them planned or expected to die as a martyr—yet all of them did. Martyrdom is not something a person anticipates or to which one readily aspires. It is an experience that God in His providence bestows on select individuals for purposes ultimately known only to Him. There seems to be no specific personal qualification for one to enter the ranks of martyrdom.

Just what is a martyr? The church has used many definitions throughout twenty-one centuries of Christian history. Some, quite broad, would allow for almost any kind of death of an individual while engaged in Christian service. Others even go as far as saying that Christians, while still alive and serving in extreme hardship circumstances, should be considered "living martyrs."

However, other definitions, like Moody's, are narrower. To put a definitive hedge around the valued memory of those who have so perished, the executive cabinet of Moody Bible Institute has adopted the following definition of a martyr:

> Those who were killed because they refused to renounce their faith or because of active opposition to their witness for Christ.[2]

Each of the men and women whose lives are recounted in this book qualifies as a martyr by this definition. All died at the hands of man while in active service on foreign soil. Some, innocently unaware of the danger of their situation, were taken quite suddenly. Others, serving while danger loomed near, had time to ponder their plight and saw their impending deaths. All were faithful and courageous till death.

It is my hope that the true-life stories told in this book will bring encouragement to all who will read and ponder the accounts of these sacrificed lives. And, if God would so choose to put another in a place of ultimate trial, that He would again grant a martyr's grace.

MARVIN J. NEWELL
Chicago

1. Taylor, F. Howard, *These Forty Years: A Short History of the China Inland Mission* (Philadelphia: Pepper Publishing Company, 1903), 395. This seems to be a direct quote from Moody given to an inquirer on the subject at the end of one of his meetings. D. L. Moody also gave a fuller explanation of what he meant in an article he wrote entitled "Sovereign Grace." "I have sometimes been asked if I had grace enough to enable me to go to the stake and die as a martyr. No; what do I want with a martyr's grace? I do not like suffering; but if God should call on me to die a martyr's death, He would give me martyrs' grace. If I have to pass through some great affliction, I know God will give me grace when the time comes; but I do not want it till it comes."(www.biblebelievers.net/salvationdoc-trine/kjcsov07.htm)

2. "Martyr Definition," adopted by executive cabinet of Moody Bible Institute (un-published document, March 2001).

To Peggy—
Faithful partner in ministry who through
the years has showered me with much grace.

THE MIDDLE EAST

Born: October 12, 1971, Downey, California

Nationality: American

Graduated from Moody: 2000

Country of Service: Lebanon

Mission: OM/Christian & Missionary Alliance

Ministry: Clinic worker

Martyrdom: 2002, age 31, Sidon

Bonnie Penner Witherall

"Help me to remember these four words: 'This is My doing'"

Bonnie is the latest, but almost certainly not to be the final, martyr of Moody Bible Institute. She was an energetic, full-of-life, risk-taking woman who loved God and loved showing His love to the unloved. But Bonnie was more than a martyr. She was a living example of how God can take a young life and mold it over time into one fully surrendered to Him, making it a delight to Himself and to others.

Bonnie walked and talked with God. Not that she was perfect, as her husband, Gary, would attest. She was a woman who over time learned to commune with God. She recorded her conversations with Him in a journal. Through it they talked back and forth with each other—like God desires all His children to do.

Total Abandon

Bonnie may well have been talking to God on that fateful November 2002 morning as she walked from her seaside apartment to the prenatal clinic where she cared for disadvantaged pregnant women. She could have been so caught up with God's presence that she was unaware of being followed by a gunman who was intent on taking her life.

Arriving at her destination, she stepped up to the entrance, turned a key, and gained entry to the small Christian complex that housed a chapel and clinic. This Christian outpost was centered in the midst of an overwhelmingly Muslim majority population and served the disadvantaged. Displaced, expectant Palestinian mothers especially took advantage of the clinic's prenatal services. Loving care rarely found anywhere else, but provided by Bonnie along with two other staff members, drew these women to the clinic.

Bonnie and Gary knew they were living and ministering in a cutting-edge, high-risk corner of God's harvest field. They lived next to an area so fanatical and violent that it was off-limits even to the local police. Their surroundings were a stark contrast from where they had come.

Two years earlier they had chosen to leave their comfortable American lifestyle in Portland, Oregon, to minister on the bleeding edge of humanity where nothing was certain except violence and great spiritual need. They did not go in ignorance. They knew the risk and understood the potential cost, but went anyway. They were certain God had called them there. They were totally abandoned to His will.[1]

Bonnie now passed along the side of the chapel and then climbed a set of stairs leading to the second-floor clinic. Turning a second key, she entered the clinic's main room. It was then that she realized someone was behind her. As she turned to greet the person she expected to be her first patient of the day, three shots rang out. Bullets fired at point-blank range struck her squarely in the head. Instantly her body fell to the floor. Streams of blood flowed from her wounds. Her spirit soared into her Savior's presence. She was now with her closest Friend.

Bonnie had not always experienced an intimate walk with God. Like a blossoming flower, her relationship with God was one that developed and grew over time until reaching full bloom.

Growing Up in the Northwest

Born in southern California, she was raised in Vancouver, Washington, where her father worked for an oil company and delighted in raising his family on a quaint hillside farm. In this idyllic setting Bonnie Penner grew up riding horses, walking fields, watching stars, and sledding across the frozen pond. In this environment she developed into a strong-spirited girl who did not shy away from adventure.

Blessed with loving parents, she learned early about God's provision of a Savior. One Sunday morning after church when Bonnie was ten years old, her mother led as she placed her trust in Christ.

However, Bonnie was a strong-willed child, and there were many times as a teenager when her willfulness got her into trouble. She was sensitive enough toward the feelings of others, though, that if she knew she had hurt or offended someone, she would ask forgiveness and make things right. She went through emotional highs and lows and spiritual ups and downs, but was learning to let God have His way. God's molding was refining her stubborn, willful character.

Preparation and Life Partner

Following high school Bonnie placed herself in another of God's molds—training at the Moody Bible Institute. A few months of study with Torchbearers in southern Germany helped her gain a deeper appreciation for God and His Word. Moody became her school of choice for further learning and character shaping.

Not all was smooth sailing at Moody. While there she experienced struggles with doubt and rebellion that brought her close to jettisoning her relationship with God altogether.

In the end, though the process was excruciating, God won her heart. Totally surrendered from that point on, she never questioned God's plan for her and His presence in her life.

It was then that she began her regular intimate times with God:

Father, I want most of all to be completely surrendered to You. Lord, more than anything I need Your fellowship . . . If there is something in my life that is keeping me from experiencing You in a deeper way, forgive me. I need You. Lord, create in me a clean heart. Reveal to me even now where I need to change to be more like You![2]

In a beautiful wedding, Bonnie was married to classmate Gary Witherall in 1997. Despite a happy marriage and successful professional careers in Portland for both of them over the next three years, the mission-trained couple was feeling dissatisfied and out of place. They had it all—money, cars, a house—but keenly felt the emptiness of the secular mold into which the world had squeezed them. Surely God had more in store for them than this.

They began searching out ministry possibilities, but they became frustrated over several overseas ministry options they pursued that never panned out. Finally one day while on her knees pleading with God, Bonnie distinctly felt Him say to her, *I have not called you to a place; I have called you to Myself.*[3] That realization made all the difference in the world. She and Gary were now completely surrendered to whatever possibility God had for them. Bonnie could now write in her journal:

I don't know what God has for us, but I want to be available to go. . . . I feel like God has me blindfolded and is leading me along a path I don't quite understand. But I will follow Him.[4]

Sidon, Lebanon

Not long afterward, Bonnie and Gary became convinced that God was pointing them to Sidon, Lebanon. In obedience, they quit their jobs, sold their possessions, packed their bags, said their good-byes, and were off to that Mediterranean port city. Operation Mobilization in partnership with the Christian and Missionary Alliance had a strategic ministry waiting for them:

Lord, here we are in the Middle East. How many people will die in this city of Sidon today without knowing You? How can I worry about my life or Gary's life when tens of thousands of people may die and face eternal damnation today? Lord, my life is already hidden with You. I know You. I have the truth. There is nothing they can take from me![5]

In September 2001 Bonnie started working at the prenatal clinic. She struggled with God about her new job and her long desire to have her own baby.

Dear Lord, I want to first of all thank You for helping me yesterday at the clinic. I was nervous because it was my first day, but I thank You because You gave me the courage and the strength to do it! God, I just want to surrender all my plans to You today. I want to give You the complete, utter control in my life. I want to lift You high above all else.[6]

Five months later, Bonnie's walk with the Lord and fellowship with Him was deepening.

Still wrestling with the disappointment of not being pregnant, Bonnie could still say to Him:

God, You are the Lord of our circumstances. We did not come to Lebanon by accident—we are exactly where You meant for us to be. Lord, I want to worship You in the place where You've put me today. Help me to remember these four words: "This is My doing."[7]

Then as summer came, Bonnie radiantly announced to Gary that she was pregnant! Her heart was filled with inexpressible joy. What she had waited for so long was now to be a reality. She was going to have a baby! Bonnie began buying baby clothes and making all those preparations expectant mothers do before their child arrives. Since she worked at a prenatal clinic, she would compare notes about body changes and morning sickness with the others.

Disappointment and Death

But then gladness turned to sudden sadness when in August her dreams were dashed with a miscarriage. Divine molding, though painful, continued to do its work. That devastating disappointment brought the ever-trusting Bonnie into deeper fellowship with her God:

God, I know that You love me and I know that everything that happens in our lives is for our good. God, You alone know how much I wanted this baby. Thank You, Lord, that Your ways are perfect and that You love and care for me so much. God, I want to trust You again for another child. God, I want Your will to be accomplished in my life, not my own. It still hurts, God, not to have this baby, but I know it was the best for Gary and me. I want to thank You for Your mercy and kindness. Even though at the time I don't recognize it as Your mercy, I know You love us and the last thing You want to do is hurt us. God, help me to trust You. Help me to draw close to You during this time.[8]

At a time when many would have cracked, questioned, quit, or turned their backs on God, Bonnie drew ever closer to her intimate friend. He alone understood and could bring comfort.

Two months later, just days before her life was taken, Bonnie reflected on the importance of the unconditional love she was asked to give day after day at the clinic. She reminds all who would serve God by serving the poor and the weak and the oppressed with the thought:

Jesus says to us that when we give a cup of water to "the least of these" we do it unto Him. Every time someone at the clinic asks me for a cup of water I give it to them, knowing I'm giving it to someone Jesus loves and cares for.[9]

Bonnie died on that cold cement floor in a pool of blood while giving that cup of love.

Lasting Impact

Since Bonnie's death, Gary has been speaking powerfully throughout North America and Europe. He is seeking one thousand students who will become missionaries—one thousand who will fill Bonnie's shoes. After speaking in two chapel services at Moody in December 2002, dozens of students packed the front of Torrey-Gray auditorium to surrender themselves anew to Christ and His cause. At Nyack College in February 2003, the stage set up in Bowman Gym became an altar flooded with students surrendering themselves to devotion and service to Christ. This same kind of impact is being repeated again and again as Gary continues to speak in schools, churches, and youth groups, telling Bonnie's story.

To those who would ponder her selfless example, Bonnie has left a lasting challenge from her journal:

Dear Jesus, Today I read in Your Word about loving our enemies. God, we have so many enemies these days. . . . In Romans 12 You tell us not to repay anyone evil for evil, but rather to be careful to do what is right in the eyes of everybody. To live at peace with all men.[10]

1. www.fisherofmen.net, "A Tribute to Bonnie Witherall" by Greg Kernaghan.

2. Gary Witherall, *Total Abandon*, 41.

3. Ibid., 54.

4. Ibid., 55.

5. Ibid., 69.

6. Ibid., 73.

7. Ibid., 1.

8. Ibid., 85.

9. Ibid., 88.

10. Ibid., 119.

CHINA

Born: 1858, Haydenville, Massachusetts

Nationality: American

Graduated from Moody: 1892

Country of Service: China

Mission: China Inland Mission

Ministry: Bible teaching/drug rehabilitation

Martyrdom: 1900, age 42, Kao-ping, Shanxi province

Hattie J. Rice

"Salt of the earth"

As Hattie trudged barefoot and half-naked in the intense July heat, it may have dawned on her that her flight for life could end in death. Because she was starved, dehydrated, and in a state of perpetual thirst, her resolve surely wore down with every painful step her blistered feet took. She never would have thought that the people she had come to love and serve would turn so violent and cruel—treating her and her fleeing companions worse than animals. Yet, the poison of the Boxers had agitated the Chinese populace into such frenzy that there remained no place of refuge for her or any foreigner in the north-central province of Shanxi. Totally exhausted, Hattie thought she would not be able to bear up under any additional hardship. But the worst was yet to come. What a contrast the end of her life was from the beginning.

New England Upbringing

Hattie was born in 1858 in the rolling hills of western Massachusetts. The picturesque village of Haydenville where she grew up was nestled in some of the loveliest hill country in New England. As they do now, people in the 1800s would come from distances to enjoy the beautiful fall foliage of the area. It was in this setting that Hattie was nurtured in a warm Christian home. Attending the town's Congregational church with her family, she learned early her need for a Savior.

Following graduation from high school, Hattie became a schoolteacher. She took a position at the Haydenville public school and soon gained the reputation of being a loving, caring teacher. Her strong Christian character made her a positive role model for her students.

It was while she was teaching that she learned about evangelist D. L. Moody, whose fame was growing. She also heard about the two schools he had recently founded, Northfield and Mount Hermon, not more than thirty miles from her home. In 1886 Mr. Moody invited college students from around the country for a twenty-six-day training conference at Mount Hermon. From this group the Holy Spirit called one hundred to declare in writing their intent to give themselves to world evangelization. Branded the "Mount Hermon 100," they became the impetus for the formation of the Student Volunteer Movement two years later.

That was when Hattie showed up at the annual conference. In 1888 she attended the Northfield Convention where she heard Moody and other well-known speakers teach and preach on the spiritual need of the world. Hudson Taylor was one of the speakers, giving a passionate plea for the unreached millions of China. His appeal so gripped Hattie that she went back to her home a changed woman. She now had no other desire but to follow God's call to China.

Obstacles and Preparation

Back in Haydenville, Hattie encountered obstacle after obstacle that threw her into times of discouragement. On the one hand, she continued in her teaching role that she loved so much, but on the other, she continued to feel keenly God's call to China. Yet she did not have the means or opportunity to go to college for the training needed. It was at this time of crisis that a friend came to her and suggested she attend Moody's Bible school in Chicago. She was even given the assurance that her church would provide the necessary means of making her education possible. Hattie was delighted and now confident that her calling would be realized. She resigned her position and made plans to go to Moody's school. In a letter of recommendation to the school, H. G. Smith, the clerk of her church, summed up her reputation by stating, "She is a lady of most estimable Christian character and one of whom it can truthfully be said is 'the salt of the earth.'"[1]

Hattie entered Moody Bible Institute (then called Chicago Bible Institute) in September 1890. She spent the next year and a half training to be a missionary, graduating in March of 1892. On her record the summary evaluation of her time at Moody succinctly stated that she was "Sensible. Faithful. Devoted. Will make an excellent missionary."[2] How prophetic those words were to be.

Having completed her studies at Moody, she left for Toronto to await appointment under the China Inland Mission (CIM). After visiting family and friends and gaining the support of her Haydenville church, she sailed for China in December of 1892.

First Years in China

Hattie arrived in Shanghai in early 1893. She began her missionary career in the city of Yang-chau, where she studied the language and culture of the Chinese people. Following that, she was assigned to the CIM work at Lu-ch'eng, Shanxi province. Along with her coworkers, the Lawsons, and another single woman, Mary Huston, the work was able to expand.

The Boxer Uprising

All was going well until the spring of 1900. At that time political events came to a crisis in China. A combination of several factors, including unfair treaties imposed by foreign powers, extreme famine caused by prolonged drought, and preferences granted to Chinese converts to Christianity and foreign Christians, fueled widespread discontent among the populace. A militant group called Boxers

United in Righteousness (originally called the Spirit Boxers) took it upon themselves to react by righting the wrongs imposed upon the Chinese citizenry. They particularly singled out foreign missionaries and Chinese Christians as their victims. The Boxers fomented mass panic and hysteria by propagating unfounded charges that the Christians and foreigners were responsible for drought-induced deaths and environmental destruction. They circulated anti-missionary rumors that these foreigners engaged in such horrendous crimes as kidnapping children, immorality, licentiousness, sorcery, and the poisoning of wells.

The Flight for Life

Spurred on by the Boxers and the Empress Dowager's edict to protect the empire and exterminate the foreigners, mad mobs began to threaten Hattie and her coworkers at Lu-ch'eng. Other nearby missionaries pursued by the mobs took refuge temporarily at Lu-ch'eng. News reached them that Yu-Hsien, the governor of the provincial city of Taiyuan, was a pro-Boxer and had interned all the missionaries of the city and surrounding areas under the guise of providing protection. Perceiving that the governor intended harm toward foreigners, the group decided it best not to go to Taiyuan to seek protection. This decision proved wise, for just two days later on July 9 the governor mercilessly beheaded thirty-three Protestant missionaries along with their children, twelve Catholic priests and nuns, and a number of Chinese Christians.

The Lu-ch'eng missionaries now realized their only hope of survival was to flee the province altogether. They would have to make a seven-hundred-mile trek on foot to the city of Hankow in Hu-peh province to the south. Hattie, her friend Mary Huston, and twelve others (including two families and their six children) decided to abandon the station and make the journey as soon as possible. Little did Hattie realize how grueling the week ahead would be.

Just before midnight on Saturday, July 7, the party secretly slipped out of Lu-ch'eng. At midmorning on Sunday they were met by a band of two hundred men who had come out of the village ahead of them. They robbed the missionary party of all they had, even stripping them of their very clothes. Hattie and the others were left with only Chinese trousers to pull around them. They trudged on as best they could in the full blaze of the intense July sun.

For the rest of that day and the following two the party passed through village after village where they were beaten and stoned. Since they had been robbed, they had nothing left to eat or drink, and whenever they stopped to rest, they were beaten with sticks and stoned with hard lumps of clay. They were only able to survive by drinking stagnant water from mud holes they periodically found by the roadside.

When they reached the city of Chang-tz, the mayor sent word that they were not permitted to enter. He did, however, provide them with food and water and promised carts to take them to the boundary of his county. They were given permission to sleep at the city wall, but even there they were not free from being pelted by stones. At midnight carts with escorts came out and rushed the mission party to the county boundary. They were given money to purchase food, and the carts returned to the city. Again on their own and with no protection, the missionaries wearily started out. They had not gone more than a mile before they were robbed of everything again. Once more they were without food, water, or money.

In the burning heat Hattie and the group trudged slowly forward for another day and a half. Unfriendly villagers continued to harass them every mile of the way. It was at this point that Hattie must have begun to realize that she probably would not survive the ordeal.

Exhausted, starved, thirsty, and barefoot, she knew she could not go on much longer. She was physically, mentally, and emotionally spent.

At noon on Thursday, the band of missionaries reached the city of Kao-ping. As before, after much pleading they were supplied with water, food, money, and the promise of carts. Again they were rushed at night to the county boundary and left to fend for themselves. Early the next morning they hired a cart at a nearby village for Hattie, who found it impossible to walk any farther. She and the children were placed on the cart and pulled through the village. As they reached the other end of the town, the party was stoned, beaten, and robbed.

The sky grew overcast, and rain began to fall. In the confusion of the rain and the mob striking them, the party became separated— Hattie and Mary Huston were driven back through the village in the direction from which they had just come.

Death on the Road

It was at this point that Hattie, totally worn out, broke down. She collapsed on the road, knowing that she could go no farther. The irate mob surrounded her, stripped her of the trousers and began stoning her as if she were a wounded animal that needed to die. In this madness a man ran a cart over her muddy body, intending to break her spine. Mary tried to shield Hattie from the cart and was herself half crushed by its weight.[3] She lost her own life from her injuries a month later.

The crowd continued their beating until Hattie finally lay motionless. The soft-spoken, gentle New England schoolteacher had succumbed, dying a shameful death at the hands of the crazed mob.

Perhaps no martyr recounted in this book mirrored more closely the death of Christ than Hattie Rice. She too was despised and rejected, beaten, manhandled by a mob, mistreated, jeered, abused, broken, thirsty, made a public spectacle, stripped, and endured her own "passion week." She also died on a Friday.

1. H. G. Smith to Chicago Bible Institute, Letter of Recommendation, 1890.
2. Moody Bible Institute Academic Records, Hattie Rice, 1892.
3. James and Marti Hefley, *By Their Blood,* 30–31.

Born: 1867, West Newton, Massachusetts

Nationality: American

Attended Moody: 1893–1894

Country of Service: China

Mission: China Inland Mission

Ministry: Nurse

Martyrdom: 1900, age 33, K'u-chau, Cheh-Kiang province

Josephine Elizabeth Desmond

"It is such a joy to find 'other sheep' in these out-of-the-way places"

The contrast between two people could not have been more pronounced. The one had all the advantages of an Asian royal palace; the other had been raised in the poverty of an Irish-American home. One was the empress of China itself, the other a newly arrived common guest to that country. One was the conniving ruler of a long-standing dynastic family, the other a devout nurse from New England. One was aged, nearing the end of her rule, the other spry and young, just starting out on life's venture. One wielded the power and authority of a despotic throne; the other selflessly ministered with a servant's heart.

By the decree of one the other would die—but her death would eventually discredit and lead to the demise of the powerful other. Empress Dowager and Josephine Desmond. Two women could not have been more opposite. Yet their lives would affect each other and the cause of Christ in China at the turn of the twentieth century.

Early Years

Empress Dowager (Tz'u-hsi), as head of the Ch'ing dynasty, was already ruling China in her first of three reigns when Josephine Desmond was born in West Newton, Massachusetts, in 1867. Josephine grew up in an Irish-Catholic home. When she was a teenager she was led to personal faith in Christ.

As a young believer, Josephine had a longing to be educated in the fundamentals of her newfound faith. A friend told her of D. L. Moody's school for girls at Northfield, and she decided that was the place for her. This all-girls' school, born out of Moody's compassion for the underprivileged, was especially meant for girls like her. Josephine had no trouble gaining entry based on her need.

Josephine spent five years at Northfield and in 1889 had an experience that would decidedly affect the direction of her life. Robert Speer, a young spokesman for the Student Volunteer Movement, who was later to become a noted missionary statesman, visited the school. He spoke to the students about the spiritual needs of peoples in the regions beyond their own country and of the plight of the unevangelized. Through his messages the voice of God came so clearly to Josephine that she committed herself to foreign missionary service. Her decision was so unwavering that it would be one on which she would never renege. By the end of her time at Northfield two years later, Josephine had developed into an attractive young woman with but one passion—to serve the Lord as a missionary.

Study in Chicago

Finished with Northfield, Josephine went west to Chicago to attend Moody Bible Institute (then called Chicago Bible Institute) to study for missionary service. In a letter of recommendation to the Institute, the headmistress of the Northfield school relayed that Josephine "is a very earnest, faithful, hardworking student, not brilliant but conscientious, and we think she might do well in some lines of Christian work."[1] Josephine entered MBI on a scholarship in September 1893. Trained under R. A. Torrey and the other faculty, she finished with a certificate the following summer. The evaluative statement on her MBI record simply states, "Sweet character. Had been reared a Catholic, earnest and devoted."[2]

Testing and Preparation

Feeling compelled to go to China, yet knowing she lacked ministry experience, Josephine decided to work among Native Americans in South Dakota. She boarded a train in Chicago heading west and soon joined a Miss Kennedy at a dilapidated rural school in South Dakota. This time of trial on the American frontier was important to Josephine—she wanted to test her faith and prove her loyalty to Christ in a hardship environment. She did just that.

After two years she felt she had proven to herself that she had the mettle to become a foreign missionary. She took a train back to Chicago and then went on to Toronto to offer herself to the China Inland Mission. While in Toronto she studied nursing with the purpose of using that as her main skill in China. Congruent with that training, she spent two years as an urban missionary, giving of herself to the poor of the city. She readily identified with these under-privileged people, having experienced the same kind of life while growing up. When the two years were completed, the mission directors felt she was qualified and accepted her into the mission. In December 1898 she boarded a ship to China.

First Year in China

Arriving in China in early 1899, Josephine's first months were at the CIM internship program in Yang-chau, the first stop for all new missionaries. Josephine adjusted well and was soon appointed to Cheh-kiang province to work at the Shiao-shan CIM station. However, soon after she arrived, the station was temporarily closed because the other missionaries had gone home for leave. Josephine was then reassigned to K'u-chau under the direction of veterans Baird and Agnes Thompson.

Upon arrival in K'u-chau, Josephine dived right into the work. With the enthusiasm of youth she brought a measure of vibrancy to the ministry. She spent her days divided between learning the Chinese language and giving nursing care at the mission clinic. For a year she and her colleagues worked together in harmony. All was peaceful around them, without a hint of trouble. Josephine felt useful and secure.

One of the last letters she wrote, a month before her martyrdom, gives a glimpse into her ministry heart. "I have been to several of the out-stations this spring. I am with the Lins, and they are so kind and have helped me much in learning to talk. Mr. Lin went with Miss Sherwood and me to places round about, we had the Bible-woman with us. The people came in crowds and listened well. In one place an old woman believed from the first and stayed with us till she had learned a prayer. It is such a joy to find the 'other sheep' in these out-of-the-way places. My limited knowledge of medicine and my small supply have been taxed. Poor people, it is sad to see so much suffering."[3]

Rebellion in Cheh-kiang

Meanwhile, at the imperial palace in Beijing, trouble was brewing. China's relations with foreign powers were moving from bad to worse, as the country feared that the foreigners in the country would influence the people. The government leaders saw this influence as a loss of control over their own people. In a desperate attempt to stem foreign influences, in early July 1900 the Empress Dowager issued the infamous secret edict that was telegraphed all over China:

> All foreigners must be killed;
> though fleeing homeward, kill them.[4]

This edict gave license to an already fomenting Boxer movement bent on capturing and killing foreigners in all parts of China. Xenophobia now ran rampant across the country. In Cheh-kiang province the secret Kiang-san Vegetarian society, an offshoot of the

Boxers, now had its excuse to launch its antiforeign and anti-Christian vengeance. They stirred up crowds into antiforeigner violence.

In response, three hundred federal soldiers were sent to K'uchau to protect the city magistrate and the missionaries from the rebellious group. However, they arrived without firearms and were thus useless against the agitated mobs. At first the missionaries were unsuspecting of any danger to themselves. But within days Josephine and her coworkers realized that their lives were in jeopardy. Rioting mobs became larger and increasingly aggressive.

On July 20 in his last letter describing the tense and increasingly hopeless situation, Baird Thompson wrote, "God, our Father, take care of us, or take us."[5] The following day God would do just that—take them to Himself. Early in the morning an unmanageable crowd attacked the mission station, looting and destroying everything in sight. Thompson tried to protect the missionaries and property under his care. In the process he was bashed in the head and received a severe wound. Josephine went to his aid, nursing the wound.

However, the two other single ladies made a run to the city magistrate for protection. They secretly made their way through narrow back streets, but upon arrival at the magistrate's court they caught sight of the magistrate himself being beheaded. Chinese friends pulled them aside in the nick of time and directed them to a secret hiding place. They hid out there for three days before being discovered and also killed.

The Massacre

Meanwhile back at the mission station, the mob had become distracted by a threat from another group of insurrectionists and had moved to the city wall to guard it. This diversion gave Josephine and the Thompsons a couple of hours of respite from danger. Josephine cleaned and bandaged Thompson's wound, gave him medicine for pain, and then together with Mrs. Thompson waited beside him and prayed. But the lull was short-lived. In the afternoon the mob returned to the station in a greater frenzy.

American philosopher and poet Ralph Waldo Emerson once stated, "A mob is a society of bodies voluntarily bereaving themselves of reason and traversing its work. The mob is man voluntarily descending to the nature of the beast."[6] The frenzied wrath of a rampaging mob is what Josephine along with the others experienced in their final moments.

Finding the missionaries taking shelter in the house, the crowd smashed in the front door. Seizing Baird Thompson, they rushed him outside, killing him in the courtyard. Reentering the house, they murdered Mrs. Thompson and her two children in front of Josephine. Then the mob turned on her and clubbed her to death as well. An eyewitness later said that all were killed quickly without experiencing prolonged suffering. The house, chapel, and other premises were looted and destroyed. The bricks of the mission buildings were pried out and taken to repair the city wall. The mission station was left in total devastation. The missionary bodies were left where they lay. This horrid scene of death and destruction would be repeated many times during the few short weeks the Boxers had their way.

A Final Contrast

Josephine, the devoted nurse, stayed loyally at her post assisting her fellow workers till the end. She ended up serving only one year before being killed because of Empress Dowager's wrath.

As for Empress Dowager, when confronted by counter-Boxer forces, she ran for her life. After a flight from the palace, she was captured and forced to make amends for what she had unleashed against the foreigners. Two years after the rebellion she returned to Beijing and eventually recovered the throne. However, she never wielded the power and influence she had had before her infamous antiforeign edict. Nor was she ever able to shake the stigma of ordering hundreds of innocent foreigners like Josephine Desmond to be mercilessly killed. Only grudgingly did she grant the right of missionaries to again work throughout her land. She died as a miserable elderly woman in 1908.

> *The tyrant dies and his rule is over;*
> *the martyr dies and his rule begins.*
> –Søren Kierkagaard[7]

1. Evelynn S. Hall to Chicago Bible Institute, 1893, 1.

2. Moody Bible Institute Academic Records, Josephine Desmond.

3. Marshall Broomhall, *Martyred Missionaries of the China Inland Mission,* 189.

4. F. Howard Taylor, *These Forty Years,* 397.

5. Broomhall, 184.

6. Ralph Waldo Emerson, "Compensation."

7. R. Daniel Watkins, *An Encyclopedia of Compelling Quotations,* 476.

Born: January 8, 1868, Waterloo, Iowa

Nationality: American

Attended Moody: 1894

Country of Service: China

Mission: American Presbyterian Board

Ministry: Medical doctor

Martyrdom: 1905, age 37, Lien-chou, Kwangsi province

Eleanor E. Chesnut, MD

"I am so fond of the people"

The anvil of hardship prepares one best for the rigors of adverse ministry experiences. Hardship and privation seem to be all Eleanor Chesnut had known her entire life. Probably no other martyr of Moody had a more disadvantaged childhood, deprived upbringing, and then austere calling than that of Dr. Eleanor Chesnut.

Early Education

Eleanor was born into a poor frontier family on the flat prairie of Iowa near the town of Waterloo on January 8, 1868. Her father abandoned her mother at the time of her birth. Then, when Eleanor was just three, her mother died, leaving her an orphan. For a while neighbors took the child in before she was passed off to a poor aunt in the backwoods of Missouri. Her aunt raised her through her early teen years. From the time that Eleanor could understand her impoverished situation, she resented it deeply. She was a miserable person and was miserable to be around. Nevertheless, although poor by economic standards, Eleanor was rich in intelligence. Her mental acumen was so impressive that at age fifteen she was admitted to Park College (now Park University) in Parkville, Missouri.

The college, situated in a scenic setting at a picturesque bend in the Missouri River, was a stark contrast to the circumstances that Eleanor experienced as an impoverished student. With barely enough money to manage, she skimped and starved to get through the academic program.

Working her way through to pay her bills, she was also a child of charity, wearing secondhand clothes that had been donated to the school for students of limited means. Most of the time she was bitter toward God because of her economic plight. Her inner feelings of resentment would not even allow her to express gratitude for the kindness that was extended. Her unusual intelligence, however, kept her excelling in her studies. She was the smartest of all students.

Over time, the religious atmosphere of the school began to have an impact on Eleanor. Eventually she surrendered herself to Christ. This decision radically changed her perspective on life and toward God. Could it be that God had gifted her with a brilliant mind coupled with hardship for a special reason—to serve Him in a unique way? The more she pondered that question, the more she felt God was calling her as a medical missionary to some hardship area of the world.

Further Preparation

After receiving her diploma from Park College, Eleanor set out to prepare herself as a medical missionary. She was accepted to the Nurses' Training School of Illinois to become a nurse. However, when her teachers became aware of her keen intelligence, she was given an opportunity that only a select group of women were granted. Eleanor was admitted to Northwestern University Women's Medical College of Chicago to study to become a physician.

She was still a young girl with very little means, but by sheer determination and frugality she was able to put herself through medical school, determined to become a missionary doctor—one of the first women to do so. To achieve this goal, she lived in an attic and mostly ate oatmeal. Meanwhile, she was so skilled at doctoring that she was granted the distinction of attending to poet and author Oliver Wendell Holmes during his final illness. He died in 1894, the same year she graduated from Northwestern.

Realizing her need for some formal Bible training before going overseas, Eleanor enrolled at Moody Bible Institute in May of that same year. She took the short course and completed it four months later. The summary statement on her record gives an insightful window into her reputation: "Very attractive, fine mind, needs dangerous experiences."[1] The assessment that she needed dangerous experiences indicates her willingness to serve the cause of Christ in whatever adverse situation she may be so led. Young Dr. Chesnut was staying true to her earlier commitment.

Since Eleanor's church background from her years at Park College was Presbyterian, she found it natural to apply to the American Presbyterian Board. She expressed a preference to serve in Siam, but stated she was willing to serve wherever the mission needed her. Even though she was still rather young and inexperienced, the board considered her well qualified. They told her she was most needed for their work in south China, and she agreed to go.

First Years in China

Eleanor was twenty-six years old when she arrived in China at the end of 1894. She was assigned to an area not far from Hong Kong. Her first years were to be spent in language study, but her reputation as a medical doctor forced her to divide her time caring for the sick as well. For four years she worked alongside other Presbyterian missionaries at a station near the border of Hunan. This was a season that helped transform the shy, sensitive, and, some say, rather difficult girl into a tender, compassionate missionary.

By 1898 Eleanor had shown herself as an able doctor to the extent that she was asked to open a new medical work in Lien-chou, Kwangsi province. This new location was three hundred miles up the Bei-Jiang River from Guangzhou (Canton), where the mission was setting up an isolated hospital. For months she worked alone, responsible for the outpatients and up to thirty inpatients at a time. The facilities were inadequate, the medicines meager, and she had few capable supporting staff personnel. Having no operating room, she was forced to do surgeries in her bathroom. At one time she had no choice but to amputate the leg of a native worker. But the wound would not heal properly, and the stump was in need of a skin graft to close it. A day later Eleanor was seen limping with new scars on her own leg. A nurse later revealed that this dedicated young doctor had removed skin from her own leg to graft onto the leg of the patient.[2]

By 1900 additional medical help had arrived. This allowed Eleanor to devote more time to female patients. She also supervised the building of a hospital especially for the care of women. Some of the funds needed came from supporters, but the rest came from her own pocket. Again, reaching back into her early experiences of privation, she lived on $1.50 a month so that the rest of her salary could be used to buy bricks for building the new facility. When the mission board became aware of what she was doing, they offered to pay her back. But Eleanor would have nothing to do with that. She refused the money, saying, "It would spoil all my fun."[3]

The summer of 1900 was an ominous time for foreigners in China as the Boxer Rebellion spread its terror across the country. Many missionaries in other places were indiscriminately being killed. In the face of this danger Eleanor refused to leave her post. She wrote a friend back in the States, "I don't think we are in any danger, and if we are, we might as well die suddenly in God's work as by some long-drawn-out illness at home."[4] The crisis passed with minimal threat to Eleanor. Eventually the mission forced her to take a break. In 1902, after eight years of uninterrupted service, she left China on her first and only furlough.

Back in the States

Eleanor made good use of her break back in the States. Her time was spent speaking about her work in China, raising funds for the hospital and chapel, giving missionary talks, and doing some graduate study in Chicago along the way. She was determined to take the most advanced medical knowledge back to China to best help the people she had come to love. She also took the opportunity to stop at Moody, relating her work to the students. With new funds and supplies in hand, she returned to China the following year.

Death of the Doctor

Back in Lien-chou Eleanor continued the work where she had left off. The mission, knowing her to be a capable and brilliant missionary, asked if she would consider the position as head of the larger and more prestigious women's hospital in Hunan. She declined, saying, "It would be a mistake for me to leave Lien-chou. I am acquainted with the people there, their dialect, diseases, faults, virtues, and other points. I am so fond of them; I don't think I could ever have quite the same feeling of affection for any other people."[5] Yet those same people would be the ones who would shortly take her life.

The day of October 29, 1905, began as any other. Eleanor and the other missionaries were busy attending to patients at the hospital. The day began as a typical one, a day they could not know would end in a horrible tragedy. The Chinese were in the midst of celebrating the Buddhist holiday Ta Tsin. Dr. Machle, one of Eleanor's colleagues, had insisted that a mat shed connected with this "idolatrous ceremony" be removed from the mission property. Local officials consented to remove it, but at the objection of some of the citizens who were offended that their culture had been violated. These in turn were able to incite a menacing mob to march on the mission property. Eleanor, sensing the danger, slipped away from the hospital to plead to the local authorities for help. She could have escaped harm altogether by staying where she was, but instead rushed back to assist her coworkers.

Meanwhile the mob had rushed onto the hospital premises. They found Dr. Machle, his wife and child, and Reverend and Mrs. John Peale trying to flee. The Peales were new missionaries who had just arrived the previous day. The half-crazed crowd chased down the fleeing missionaries and killed all five next to the river in front of a Buddhist temple. They had just finished the killing when Eleanor returned, rushing to help them.

Seizing her, the mob pushed her down the temple steps to the foot of a large tree. She freed herself and sat down on a mound to see what they would do. At that moment she noticed a little boy in the crowd with an ugly gash on his head incurred by the frenzied throng. In the midst of the mayhem she called him over, tore off the hem of her dress, and bound his wound "with skilled, kind fingers that did not tremble,"[6] as a witness would later report. This final act of kindness did nothing to placate the incensed mob.

They waited until she was through, then converged on her again. Four ruffians rushed upon her, dragged her down the steep bank, and threw her into the river. Then one jumped into the water and stabbed her three times—once in the neck, once in the chest, and once in the abdomen. About ten minutes later they brought her body to shore.[7] Eleanor's life of hardship was now ended.

Lasting Impact

The martyrdom of Dr. Chesnut not only had a profound impact on many at that time, but still continues to do so today. A search on the Internet reveals that her sacrifice is mentioned repeatedly in sermons that espouse self-denial and sacrificial love. Probably the most moving tribute that was ever paid to Eleanor's selfless devotion to Christ was written by Helen Barrett Montgomery five years later. In her book *Western Women in Eastern Lands* she wrote:

> Thus one of the choice spirits of American womanhood laid down her life for the redemption of China. As God lives, her sacrifice shall not be in vain. Other college girls will feel their eyes wet and their hearts hot as they read her story. Out of her life laid down shall spring many lives consecrated to hard service in unlovely places. The whole world will perceive that a box of ointment, very precious, has once more been poured over the feet of the Savior and filled all the room with its perfume.[8]

1. Moody Bible Institute Academic Records, Eleanor Chesnut.

2. Robert Speer, *Servants of the King,* 104.

3. Ruth Tucker, *Guardians of the Great Commission,* 154.

4. Helen Montgomery, *Western Women in Eastern Lands,* 198.

5. Speer, 105.

6. Montgomery, 199.

7. Speer, 109.

8. Montgomery, 199.

Born: June 24, 1898, Sweden

Nationality: Swedish

Attended Moody: 1921–1922

Country of Service: China

Mission: Swedish Alliance Mission

Ministry: Church planter

Martyrdom: 1928, age 30, Fangchen

Robert Elias Blomdahl

"We must be faithful"

Some martyrs have simply been forgotten—or at least details of their lives and deaths are so sketchy that there is little hope of their being rediscovered. Robert Blomdahl was such a martyr. Since he was Swedish and served with a Swedish mission agency, official word of his murder in China took years to reach Moody Bible Institute, where he had studied for two terms and part of a third.

We are able to reconstruct only pieces of his life. We know that he was born in Jönköping, Sweden, in 1898—the same year that Ella Schenck, the first martyr of Moody, was killed. We also know he was raised on a farm, was a member of the Free Church, and came to know the Lord as his Savior at age twenty.[1]

Blomdahl arrived at Moody with minimal English but a lot of zeal. He was a free spirit who needed to take better care of his health than he did to conserve his strength. Evidently he was married, but left his wife back in Sweden during his tenure in Chicago. After ten months of study he left Moody in July of 1922.

He and Elly, his wife, went to China as missionaries not long afterwards. Regrettably, the Swedish Alliance Mission with whom he served has lost record of his service, causing all trace of his ministry and death to fall into obscurity. Fortunately, his wife wrote to MBI several years after his death, giving details that otherwise would have remained unknown.

In October 1928 Blomdahl was in Fangchen, North China, on his way to Tokota for mission meetings. He along with Filip Malmvall, another former Moody student, had taken a room overnight in a Chinese hostel. Suddenly bandits entered, catching the two off guard. With guns pointed they demanded that the men hand over their watches and money. As Blomdahl was taking his watch from his pocket, he was shot and killed on the spot. Filip Malmvall was spared.[2]

We do get a glimpse into Blomdahl's heart attitude as a missionary from his wife. She wrote, "If I would hold him back, he would say, 'No, Elly dear, we are not here for the pleasure but for Christ's sake and thus we must be faithful.' "[3]

What Is Martyrdom?

A question arises because of the death of Robert Blomdahl that could be asked of similarly declared martyr deaths. Does the seemingly senseless murder of a missionary in a robbery duly qualify him as a martyr? In their book *By Their Blood*, James and Marti Hefley help answer that question. Some martyrs may be excluded from being identified as a martyr by dying in an accident, during a robbery, or other means that could have happened anywhere, not only the mission field. Certainly, the line is hard to draw. However, we need to remember that someone such as Robert Blomdahl was where he was because of his devotion to Christ.

Second, we need to avoid the oversimplification that martyrs always die strictly and directly *for* their testimony of Christ. When all the details become known, it is apparent that many Christian martyrs die in circumstances *related* to their witness, not fully because of it.[4] While engaged in ministry, they die at the hands of man, in contrast to, say, having an accident. For this reason Robert Blomdahl and others are counted among martyrs for the cause of Christ.

1. "Moody Bible Institute Martyrs," no date, 2.
2. Ibid.
3. Ibid.
4. James and Marti Hefley, *By Their Blood*, 9.

Born: April 3, 1899, Shanghai, China

Nationality: Swedish

Attended Moody: 1928

Country of Service: China

Mission: Scandinavian Alliance Mission

Ministry: Church planter, relief director

Martyrdom: 1932, age 33, near Xi'an, Shaanxi province

Gustaf David Nathaniel Tornvall

"Made in China, died in China"

Gustaf saw a ride in the car of Henry Ekvall, an American international salesman for Ford Motor Company, as a rare treat. Hardly ever in all his years in China had he had the opportunity to ride in an automobile, especially in the interior of the far northwest. But time was beginning to change the way of life for even the common people of Kansu (now Gansu) province. Gravel roads were being carved into the countryside where, for centuries, people confined their travel to narrow footpaths and bumpy cart trails.

A perceptive missionary who sensed the economic value of such transportation progress for his fellow people, Gustaf had volunteered his services as a relief director to manage funds paid to the Chinese laborers who were building the roads. In addition, he viewed the money made by the people he supervised as a means of providing income for themselves at a time when a great famine had crippled the economy.

Henry Ekvall, on the other hand, was in China for the sole purpose of making a profit. As a salesman for Ford, he wanted to grab exclusive rights to the fresh market in this remote part of the country. He had known Gustaf from earlier years and saw the experienced missionary as just the ticket he needed to further his travels as he made contact with prospective buyers in the northwest. Having just finished business in the Kansu region, he now needed to travel back to his base in Xi'an, the ancient capital of China, two hundred miles to the southeast.

Gustaf also needed to get to Xi'an to purchase equipment and supplies for the work crews he was supervising. With up to forty thousand daily workers carving out new roads, he was looking for a safe way to transport the large amount of funds he was carrying to purchase supplies required to keep such a mammoth labor force working. Henry was happy to discover that Gustaf, who knew the culture and language like a native, was going his direction. What better companion to have along, as he too carried a substantial amount of money and even some gold. As they set out on that fateful trip on July 22, 1932, neither man knew the danger that awaited them farther down the road. Nor did they realize this would be their last ride.

Early Childhood

Gustaf Tornvall was born to missionary parents in Shanghai on April 3, 1899. His parents, David and Therese Tornvall, were among the first missionaries to enter China under the China Alliance Mission (later Scandinavian Alliance Mission and now TEAM). Inspired by the passionate plea of missionary statesman Fredrick Franson, the young couple had arrived in 1891 in the first wave of missionaries of this new society. Following language study on the coast, they turned their eyes to the interior, pioneering the work in Pingliang, Kansu province, in 1895. It was in this environment of new beginnings that Gustaf was born.

Gustaf was "made in China"—conceived, born, raised, and immersed in that environment to such an extent that he was more Chinese than Western. In 1902, at the age of three, he had a special benediction placed upon him when the much-revered Hudson Taylor visited the Tornvall home. Laying his hand on Gustaf's head, he prayed, "Lord, I claim this little child of Thee for China."

Growing up, Gustaf's closest friends were his Chinese playmates. He spoke Chinese better than English or even Swedish (his parents' language). But even with all the godly influences of home, parents, and mission exerting themselves, Gustaf had little desire to follow the beliefs of his parents.

That commitment/decision would not happen until later when he was a student at the China Inland Mission School in Chefoo. As a teen-ager, Gustaf was sent there for his high school training. While there, at the age of sixteen, he gave his heart to Christ and consecrated his all to the Lord.

The Novice Missionary

Following graduation, Gustaf went home to his parents' work at Pingliang. Although only seventeen, he thrust himself into the work at his father's side, helping to lighten the burden his father was carrying in the multifaceted work of the station. To provide education, there was a mission school; to promote spiritual life, a church; and to offer medical care, a hospital. All these ministries demanded the undivided time and efforts of the Tornvalls.

One day as his father was baptizing a large group of converts, Gustaf also entered the waters to receive the rite. His father, moved to tears, baptized his one and only son who had taken so long to receive for himself the gospel message that the senior Tornvall had been propagating to the Chinese for over two decades.

Not long afterward, Gustaf was also designated a missionary with the Scandinavian Alliance Mission (now TEAM) and worked hard to further the gospel among the people he had grown to love and call his own. The church, hospital, and school had all developed and were tending to the welfare of the poor and disadvantaged people of the area. Gustaf proved himself so dependable that in 1923 when he was just twenty-five, his father left him in charge of the work while he took the rest of the family back to Sweden and the States for a break from the work.

In the States

It was at that time that sorrow and trouble struck Gustaf in a way he could never have foreseen. While in the midst of the work, word reached him that his father had suddenly passed away shortly after arriving in Sweden. At the same time he received urgent word from the Swedish consul in Shanghai advising all expatriate personnel to immediately evacuate inland areas due to increasing civil unrest and disturbance. Foreign governments did not want a repeat of the heartless slaughter of their citizens that had happened during the Boxer rebellion two decades earlier. Heartbroken and in need of rest himself, Gustaf decided it was a good time to leave the country to visit his newly widowed mother and six sisters, who had taken up residence in Chicago.

While in Chicago, Gustaf took advantage of the time with his family to acquire some theological training. He knew that with the passing of his father much of the spiritual ministry of the mission would fall to him. He entered Moody Bible Institute's evening school in 1928. Gustaf was single-minded and had but one goal—to get his education as quickly as possible and then return to China. A remark on his Moody record bears this out, tersely stating: "does not expect to remain."[1] Gustaf studied at Moody for the full academic year of September 1927–July 1928.

While Gustaf was studying, word came from China that the interior was gradually opening again to foreigners. Gustaf's desire was to be back helping the people he knew best. He returned by mid-1928. Fluent in the language and knowledgeable of the culture, Gustaf went even a step further of identifying with the people by dressing much of the time like the native Chinese.

Work of Compassion

Not long after he resumed his work in Pingliang, a great famine fell on western China. It was a time of intense human agony. Gustaf witnessed terrible suffering and physical hardship among the people and felt compelled to engage in some kind of effort to help. Attending to the overwhelming needs of the people, it was not long before Gustaf himself experienced mental and spiritual suffering as he saw friends and acquaintances painfully die from starvation. The situation was so overwhelming that he came to realize there was little he could do in and of himself. Then an offer came that would give an opportunity in a substantial way to help alleviate the suffering.

The China International Famine Relief Commission initiated a program of giving the stricken people work. The commission would pay laborers to build roads that could be used by motorized vehicles. Since it paid the laborers in cash, they needed a trustworthy manager to handle the funds. Gustaf was asked to serve as supervisor for the Kansu region. Sensing the relief the work program would bring the people, Gustaf gladly accepted. In this role Gustaf gained the admiration of the people and a wide reputation. "He was able, cautious and warmhearted, and a true missionary. Farmers and officials had the greatest respect for him," said O. J. Todd, the chief engineer.[2]

Gustaf continued in church development along with relief work. He visited and supervised the work of his fellow missionaries. Around this time, his sister Sofia came to join the work. The special treat of having her there was enhanced when she fell in love with his coworker and friend Earl Peterson. Gustaf performed their marriage ceremony.

While supervising the road projects, Gustaf made it his habit to preach the gospel to the work crews. He never lost sight of the main reason he was in China. But he made certain his relief efforts did not make superficial "rice Christians" out of the people, as had been done in other parts. Gustaf made it clear that they need not attend church in return for being provided with much-needed employment.

Vanished!

The fateful day came in July of 1932 when Gustaf innocently caught that automobile ride with Henry Ekvall. Gustaf was aware that potential danger loomed in the form of lawlessness, and that thought most likely was why he felt it more prudent to drive from Pingliang to Xi'an with Ekvall. Just days earlier he had received an urgent telegram from the US Department of State, communicated by William Castle, undersecretary, which stated:

> Due to the growth of banditry and other forms of lawlessness it is felt that American citizens are jeopardizing their lives by remaining in the affected areas. The Department strongly urges that American missionary organizations which have representatives stationed in the areas . . . consider the advisability of withdrawing such representatives to places where conditions afford a reasonable means of safety.[3]

Forewarned and well aware of potential danger, Gustaf, Henry, and two others started their two-hundred-mile journey by car. They traveled most of that day and spent the night at the village of Li Chuan on the banks of the Wei River. The following morning they crossed the river by ferry. A ferry crossing in the opposite direction had an English Baptist missionary on it, and Gustaf carried on a conversation with him until they were out of earshot. That was the last time they were seen by anyone acquainted with them. Gustaf and his companions were never heard from again. They seemed to have simply vanished!

The fate of Gustaf can only be pieced together by fairly reliable Chinese accounts of those who encountered them farther along the way. According to these stories, just a few miles north of Xi'an, six

Chinese soldiers stopped the car. Villagers saw the men taken by the soldiers to a house where they were detained for the rest of the day. It soon became clear that these were renegade soldiers out to rob the foreigners. We don't know what Gustaf may have said to his captors as he tried to reason with them for his life. But one can envision him pointing out that he was "a son of the soil," "a religious teacher," or "there helping the people." However, all was to no avail.

At dusk the car was driven out into a field, its headlights drawing the notice of a local farmer who was still working close by. Sensing something sinister, the farmer kept a watch but did not get too near, as there were about thirty armed men on horseback escorting the vehicle. Moments later he heard a volley of gunshots which startled him. He then heard someone cry, "There is still one more," and then two more shots. It seems certain that Gustaf, Ekvall, and the other two had been summarily executed. Their bodies were never recovered.[4]

When news of Gustaf's murder reached Pingliang, it evoked an outcry and expression of sorrow so deep that all levels of the community decried his death with great indignation. Such was the stature and affection he had gained within their hearts. As coworker O. J. Todd summarized upon hearing word of Gustaf's death:

> Brave, indeed, are those who pour their lives into the mission fields of Shensi and Kansu these days. Many have suffered and given up their lives, but we wonder why so able and fine a man as Tornvall should have been taken so young.[5]

1. Moody Bible Institute Academic Records, Gustaf Tornvall.
2. O. J. Todd, "An Outstanding Missionary," *The Missionary Broadcaster,* 8.
3. William Castle, "Official Communication from the Department of State."
4. Othilie Olsen, "More about Tornvall's Death," *The Evangelist,* 11.
5. Todd, Ibid.

Born: January 18, 1907, Paterson, New Jersey

Nationality: American

Graduated from Moody: 1932

Country of Service: China

Mission: China Inland Mission

Ministry: Church planter

Martyrdom: 1934, age 27, Miaosheo, Anhwei province

John Cornelius Stam

"Whether by life or by death"

At the Moody Bible Institute and in its student missionary activity I was brought face to face with my own responsibility to heathen millions. The Lord laid China upon my heart, and slowly the conviction deepened that I, for one, would have no valid reason to give my Lord if I did not go where the need was so great. God's Word itself, prayer and the study of conditions in China, and my own circumstances soon left no room for doubt that the Lord was assuredly leading.[1]

So wrote John Stam in the China Inland Mission's magazine *China's Millions* as he set sail for China and, unbeknownst to him, for a martyrdom that would have a wide impact on the American Christian community for decades. His conviction that "the Lord was assuredly leading" would no doubt contribute to the supernatural fortitude he mustered as he and his new bride faced the horrors of a cruel death exacted by merciless communists two years later.

Start

John was born on a cold January day in 1907 in Paterson, New Jersey. He died on a cold December day in China twenty-seven years later. The fifth child in a family of six sons and three daughters, he was the son of immigrant parents from Holland who had met and married after arriving in the States. John's parents were devout Christians who made it their duty to bring their children up in a godly home. He was taken to church religiously and sent to the Christian Grammar School, and then as a teen lent a hand in helping his father run the Star of Hope Mission. His father had founded this mission out of compassion for underprivileged people in the community. John's conversion was neither early nor automatic. However, at the age of fifteen the preaching of a blind evangelist speaking at the mission had an impact on him. This experience, along with his studies at a small business college the same year, led to his decision to accept Christ for himself.

Surrender

Following business school, John began a promising career in New York City during the prosperous "roaring twenties." His office windows overlooked the harbor. Over time he was drawn to the international freighters and ocean liners that brought him in contact with foreign peoples. Periodically strolling through Chinatown on his way to and from work, he began to have a burden to reach these people with the love of Christ.[2] To the chagrin of his employers and surprise of his coworkers, John turned his back on his career when he resigned his business position to serve God. Knowing he needed Bible training, he made plans to enter the Moody Bible Institute. However, he would do so under one stipulation—that God alone would provide for his needs as long as he was a student.

Struggles

Refusing any help from his parents or friends, he took his savings and entered Moody in September 1929. Although he did well in his studies, John struggled in other areas. He strove to live the victorious Christian life on a plane he hadn't experienced before. In a letter to his brother he confided, "My only trouble is myself."[3] In his diary he wrote:

> I have long been praying that God will keep me from foolishly looking for experiences such as others have—each life is planned separately, I know. But I could not fail to notice that

in many experiences and in many spiritual struggles and
strivings there are likenesses. I have . . . a fearfulness of com-
mitting one's self to paper, for fear of what others might think
should they chance to read it later.[4]

John struggled to support himself financially. America was now in
the midst of the Great Depression, and money was hard to come by.
Yet he resolutely refused help from others in order to place full faith
in God and His provision. Writing about his experience of joining a
friend in his car for a holiday trip back to Paterson, he mentions how
tight things were for him:

> I had told Tom I was going with him, but I didn't have any
> money and couldn't even buy a warm pair of socks for the
> trip home in the car. Then, one night, I pulled on one of the
> four shirts I had been planning to take home with me, and it
> ripped. I did not want to take home a mended shirt, for
> Mother would guess that finances were low, and I did want to
> see the Lord's provision, as a test of what His care would be
> in times to come. I went out by the lake, feeling a bit blue and
> downcast, and found myself thinking, "Well, it's all right to
> trust the Lord, but I wouldn't mind having a few dollars in my
> pocket." A few minutes later, just as I was crossing Michigan
> Boulevard—and jaywalking too—I picked up a five-dollar bill
> from the street. Oh, what a rebuke it was from the Lord! Just
> one of those gentle rebukes the Lord can so wonderfully give
> us. The five dollars was beautifully acceptable, even though it
> was wet. I dried it out and next day visited Montgomery Ward's
> bargain counter and bought a couple of shirts and a good
> warm pair of socks, just the thing for the trip. I am wearing
> those same socks still, and every time I pull them on, these

cold nights, they preach a sermon on the Lord's wonderful power to provide, whatever my future needs may be.[5]

John struggled to be a bold and consistent Christian witness. The November 21, 1930, entry in his journal says,

> While I am having training this term in learning to trust Him alone—God grant that I may learn it fully—last term I had some severe struggles and lessons in self-denial. I remember promising the Lord that I would deny myself after refusing to pass out tracts. What misery I had, when I did not want to deny myself for His sake. God grant that the lesson is learned, but I fear I have further installments still to come.[6]

John also struggled to find a perfect balance in his relationship with a fellow student, Betty Scott, to whom he felt drawn. They would meet together at China prayer meetings, and then she graduated from Moody a year ahead of him. She was at the China Inland Mission Home in Philadelphia when he wrote,

> Betty is in Philadelphia now, but I have not been able to write her a letter. After much searching of my heart and of the Scriptures, I feel that the Lord would be displeased at my going forward in this direction. And only last week a man came up to my room to have me type a letter for him. A former student, he told me with tears in his eyes that he had gotten out of the will of the Lord when he stopped his studies and got married. What grief he has had since. And now, while Betty and I are looking forward to the same field, I cannot move one step in her direction until I am sure that it is the Lord's directive will. I don't want to wreck her life and mine too.[7]

Lastly, John struggled to find God's direction for his life. Should he stay in the States or give himself as a missionary to China? In the end, he came to discover that full surrender to God was what was most important, and God would take it from there. "I give myself to Thee, Lord Jesus. Use me as Thy tool for Thy glory." Pondering the needs overseas, he wrote his brother Jacob,

> The Lord knows where He wants me, whether in Holland, in Paterson or some other place in the States, in China or in India. However, it does look frightfully disproportionate to see so many here in comparison with the few over yonder. We know that the Lord's work is not over-staffed here, but, as someone has said, "There are those who simply cannot go and those who are free to go. Why should both stay at home for the same work?"[8]

By the time he graduated from Moody, he was certain the Lord would have him serve in China. Chosen by his classmates to be the class speaker, he gave a rousing challenge of missions to his fellow classmates. Upon graduation from Moody, the dean wrote on John's record, "Unusual Christian character. Had the bearing mind of college or university trained man. Much natural leadership. Reflects the godly home from which he came. Enjoyed implicit confidence of all the students. Good student, consecrated Christian. He will undoubtedly be heard from."[9]

Service

After a six-week stay at the China Inland Mission in Philadelphia, John was appointed for service to China in July 1932. He immediately crossed the continent by tourist car to California. From there he sailed third class on the *Empress of Japan* with five other young men and two returning missionaries.

Upon arrival in Shanghai, John had the unexpected surprise to find that Betty was there! She had been continually in his thoughts during the long voyage, and he wondered when he would ever see her again. But God had providentially orchestrated events so the two would meet almost immediately upon setting foot in the city.

Stricken with tonsillitis while visiting her missionary parents, Betty had been forced to remain in Shanghai for a few weeks of recovery, just long enough to see John arrive. He wrote home to his parents:

> I still cannot cease praising the Lord and wondering at His goodness in bringing Betty to Shanghai and keeping her there until I came. One of the boys from Australia asked me how we had "worked" it, and it was just blessed to realize that we hadn't worked it at all. It was unplanned and unexpected, as far as we were concerned . . . to me it has been a wonderful illustration of the fact that when we do "seek first" the kingdom of God, although our efforts may be blundering, He does unstintingly add the "all things."[10]

Mustering courage, John straightaway asked Betty if she would marry him. She accepted without hesitation. They had known since their Moody days that they were meant for each other.

At that time, the CIM had a rule that engaged couples could not get married until they had spent a full year separated on the field. John and Betty soon parted ways and would not see each other again until the eve of their marriage one year later. John went by steamer up the Yangtze River to language school in Anking. Betty went the same direction but onward in Anhwei province to the work in Fowyang. It was a trying year of separation for both of them, but they persevered through it.

Finally, in October of 1933, they both made their way to Tsinan, where Betty's parents served as missionaries. After a few days together, the bridal party gathered for the wedding. On the morning of October 25 they were joined together in holy matrimony. Two lives that had been separate for so long were now one.

The Stams spent the next year in joyful bliss studying language and visiting various mission stations. Their joy was made even more complete eleven months later when Helen Priscilla was born to them. In the joy of that moment, little did they or anyone else realize the tragic fate that awaited them next.

Sacrifice

Communist activity was said to have subsided in Anhwei province, where the mission assigned the Stams to work in the city of Tsingteh. John and Betty were assured by the city magistrate that there was no danger to them, and their safety was guaranteed. After further investigation and prayer on John's part, he felt it was safe enough to move his family to Tsingteh as the mission requested. They reached the city at the end of November when the weather was beginning to turn cold. They immediately set up home in a large Chinese house and were grateful it had two stoves. But their stay would be short-lived.

Hardly had they settled in when on December 6, a battalion of Communists entered the city. The city magistrate who had promised the Stams protection was one of the first to flee. John and Betty were taken by surprise and had no time to evacuate before the Communists made it to their door. Upon entering, Betty served them tea and cakes while John calmly explained to them their peaceful intentions for being there. But the captors were in no mood for niceties. They instructed John to write the mission, demanding $20,000 in ransom money. John obliged with the following:

December 6, 1934

Tsingteh, An.

China Inland Mission

Shanghai

Dear Brethren:

My wife, baby and myself are today in the hands of the Communists, in the city of Tsingteh. Their demand is twenty thousand dollars for our release.

All our possessions and stores are in their hands, but we praise God for peace in our hearts and a meal tonight. God grant you wisdom in what you do, and us fortitude, courage, and peace of heart. He is able—and a wonderful friend in such a time.

Things happened so quickly this A.M. They were in the city just a few hours after the ever-persistent rumors really became alarming, so that we could not prepare to leave in time. We were just too late.

The Lord bless you and guide you, as for us—may God be glorified, whether by life or by death.

In Him,

John C. Stam[11]

The following morning the Communists forced the Stams along with other captives out of Tsingteh. They were force-marched across the mountains for twelve miles to the town of Miaosheo. Once there, John and Betty were hurried into the postmaster's shop and left under guard while the soldiers took over the town. John seized the opportunity to write one last letter to the mission:

December 7, 1934
Miaosheo, An.

China Inland Mission

Dear Brethren,

We are in the hands of the Communists here, being taken from Tsingteh when they passed through yesterday. I tried to persuade them to let my wife and baby go back from Tsingteh with a letter to you, but they wouldn't let her, and so we both made the trip to Miaosheo today, my wife traveling part of the way on a horse.

They want $20,000 before they will free us, which we have told them we are sure will not be paid. Famine relief money and our personal money and effects are all in their hands.

God grant you wisdom in what you do and give us grace and fortitude. He is able.

Yours in Him,
John C. Stam[12]

These final words from John showed no sign of fear, self-pity, or faltering. His deep faith, which he developed by walking closely with the Lord through the years, strengthened him as he resolutely faced whatever would come.

The Communists, finished with taking over the town, turned their attention back to their American captives. John and Betty were led to a small room, where they were guarded through the night. John was tied with ropes to a bed frame. Betty was left untied, permitting her to attend to the baby. All three were cold throughout the night because of the brisk December temperatures. One can only guess what they said to each other those few remaining hours together.

At daybreak the guards entered the room and forced John and Betty to remove their outer clothes before binding them with ropes—an ominous sign of what was ahead. With a last glance at baby Helen, the two were hustled out of the room. Barefoot, with their hands tied behind their backs, they were made a spectacle as they were marched past the townspeople who had been summoned to witness the execution. Once out of town they were led up a hill to a grove of pine trees. Taunted by their captors, they were ridiculed until the crowd could barely stand it. One Chinese believer, unable to bear the taunting any longer, stepped forward and pleaded for the Stams's lives. He was quickly beaten, and John begged for mercy for this brother—the final act of his brief missionary career.

A swift stroke of a sword severed his head from his body. Betty was then commanded to suffer the same. After a momentary tremble, she too fell to her knees. With a flash her body also sank lifeless next to her husband's. Their gruesome deed now finished, the callous soldiers forced the villagers back into town.

The Stams's bodies lay where they had fallen for the rest of the day and into the night. Under cover of darkness some believers mustered the courage to retrieve them. Baby Helen was found by some Christians the next day and secretly transported in a rice basket over the mountains for a week, eventually making it to the home of her grandparents.

Shock

The impact of the deaths of John and Betty was widespread and keenly felt, touching countless lives. Those who personally knew the couple were shocked to hear about the manner of their death. When word of the Stams's martyrdom reached Moody half a world away, the impact was profound on the student body. In a chapel service, seven hundred students rose to their feet to recommit themselves to God. Through the example of the Stams they clearly understood the implications of their decision. Many were now willing to give up personal ambitions and change the direction of their lives for the cause of Christ. The same happened at other Christian colleges. At Wheaton College, two hundred students offered themselves to Christian service [13] Churches across the country felt the same impact of the Stams's sacrifice.

Meanwhile in China, countless Chinese Christians, moved by the Stams's deaths, put away bickering and strife, rededicating themselves to the Lord. Eternity alone will tell how much was gained by the death of these two young missionaries. Certainly Christ was magnified through John and Betty Stam—both in life and in death.

1. Kathleen White, *John and Betty Stam*, 28.
2. Mrs. Howard Taylor, *The Triumph of John and Betty Stam*, 13.
3. Schuyler E. English, *By Life and By Death*, 14.
4. Taylor, 15–16.
5. English, 20.
6. Ibid.
7. Taylor, 18.
8. Ibid, 60.
9. Moody Bible Institute Academic Records, John Stam.
10. English, 57.
11. Mrs. Howard Taylor, *John and Betty Stam: A Story of Triumph*, 116–117.
12. Thomas Shaw and Dwight A. Clough, *Amazing Faith*, 125.
13. Lee S. Huizenga, *John and Betty Stam—Martyrs*, 87.

Born: February 22, 1906, Albion, Michigan

Nationality: American

Graduated from Moody: 1931

Country of Service: China

Mission: China Inland Mission

Ministry: Church planter

Martyrdom: 1934, age 28, Miaosheo, Anhwei province

Elizabeth (Betty) Alden Stam

"To live is Christ"

> Lord, I give up my own purposes and plans, all my own desires
> and hopes and ambitions and accept Thy will for my life. I give
> myself, my life, my all utterly to Thee, to be Thine forever. I
> hand over to Thy keeping all of my friendships; all the people
> whom I love are to take a second place in my heart. Fill me and
> seal me with Thy Holy Spirit. Work out Thy whole will in my
> life, at any cost, now and forever. To me to live is Christ. Amen.[1]

So wrote nineteen-year-old Betty Scott on a pledge card at America's
Keswick, the New Jersey conference center, in the summer of 1925.
Nine years after making that vow, Betty, then a young mother, would
come to understand the extent of what the "at any cost" would come
to mean one cold December day in China.

Elizabeth (Betty) Alden Scott was born in Albion, Michigan, to parents serving as home missionaries. Not long after her birth, the family of seven packed up and sailed to China, where Dr. Scott was
appointed as a Bible teacher under the Presbyterian Board, USA.
Their family motto was "Do it together." By design, Betty's parents
made all events in their missionary life family events. Work, play, reading, meals, vacationing were all done in a spirit of oneness. Her family grew so close-knit that when it was time for the children to go off to
a distant boarding school, they still maintained strong ties with one
another. As her early years passed, Betty exhibited two outstanding
gifts: learning the Chinese language and a knack for writing poetry.

As a teen at the coeducational mission school at Tungchow, Betty
grew in her appreciation of her parents. Her love for them was reflected
in a poem she wrote:

To Father and Mother

My words, dear Father, precious Mother,
    May God select from His rich store.
  I am, because you loved each other—
    O, may my love unite us more!

When I was born, brimmed the bright water,
    For pain and joy, in eyes gray-blue.
     (A tiny bud of you, a daughter;
     And yet, distinct a person too!)

As life grew bigger, I stood firmer,
    With legs apart, eyes fond and wide.
    You told me all I asked, a learner
     Who was not ever satisfied

But not content with mental culture,
    Seeing my spirit mourn in night,
  You taught the Word and Way for sinners,
    Until Christ's Spirit brought me light.

Your love for others, in each other,
Shines through the world, pain-tarnished here;
  As faithful stewards, Father, Mother,
  Your crown shall be unstained by tear.

Imagine, in God's certain heaven,
    Your children made forever glad,
  Praising the Lord for having given
    The dearest parents ever had.[2]

Their solidarity as a family was broken when the children needed to go back to America to continue their education. Betty, at age
seventeen, was about ready for college when the family's furlough
was due in 1923. For the trip home Dr. Scott decided to take the family on a six-month study/travel tour, visiting Singapore, Egypt, the
Holy Land, Greece, Italy, Switzerland, France, and England along the
way. Betty delighted in her encounter with other people's customs
and cultures, writing:

TRAVELER'S SONG

I sought for beauty on the earth,
And found it everywhere I turned;
A precious stone from Singapore
That sapphire shone and sapphire burned—
A Rajah's ransom it was worth.

Eternal grandeur brooded deep
In Egypt's pyramids of stone;
And still I smell the orange bloom,
I see the frosty stars that shone
And cooled the tranquil Nile to sleep.

I loved the skies of Italy,
The swarthy, singing boatmen there,
The Virgins of the Renaissance,
With grave, sweet eyes and golden hair—
The land of Art and Melody.

Linger long into the night
On snowy peaks the Alpine glow,

And every lake is loveliest,
And there, amid the endless snow,
I picked the edelweiss so white.

Before a Chinese gate,
The entrance to an ancient town,
I saw the men fly dragon-kites;
While, by the willows weeping down,
Their wives beat clothes, from dawn to late.

Then home I came, as though on wings,
The joy of life in heart and eyes;
For, everything was glorified—
The earth, the ocean, and the skies,
And even all the common things.[3]

Upon arrival in the States Betty entered Wilson College in Chambersburg, Pennsylvania. But she was suddenly struck with a serious illness. Inflammatory rheumatism left her heart so weak that she had to lie flat on her back for months. This trial led Betty to ponder spiritual things in a new and deeper way.

It was during summer break that she attended America's Keswick, where she surrendered her life fully to God, making her unreserved vow to Him. She also did two other things that would guide the direction of her life. For one, she made Philippians 1:21, "To me to live is Christ, and to die is gain," her life's verse. Through the years she would call on that verse often, right up to the moment of her martyrdom. The other was to begin to pray that if it was God's will, nothing would detract her from returning to China as a missionary.

With this new desire, upon leaving college she enrolled at Moody for practical missionary training. A standout among the students, she eventually was elected secretary of her graduating class. It was at this time that Betty grew in the depth of her prayer life, as revealed in her poem "Sonnet on Prayer." But she also deepened in her surrender to God. After a period of distress of soul, she wrote her father about victory in this area:

STAND STILL AND SEE

I'm standing, Lord:
There is a mist that blinds my sight.
Steep, jagged rock, front, left and right,
Lower, dim, gigantic, in the night.
Where is the way?
I am afraid!

I'm standing, Lord:
The black rock hems me in behind,
Above my head a moaning wind
Chills and oppresses heart and mind,
I am afraid!

I'm standing, Lord:
The rock is hard beneath my feet;
I nearly slipped, Lord, on the sleet.
So weary, Lord! and where a seat?
Still must I stand.

He answered me, and on His face
A look ineffable of grace,
Of perfect, understanding love,
Which all my murmuring did remove.

I'm standing, Lord:
Since Thou hast spoken, Lord, I see
Thou hast beset—these rocks are Thee!
And since Thy love encloses me,
I stand and sing.

Resolute to give herself for service in China, Betty joined the Monday-evening China prayer meetings held in the home of Mr. and Mrs. Page, representatives of the China Inland Mission (CIM). During her second year she could not help but notice a new and appealing face at the prayer meetings, a student named John. Over time John discreetly made overtures toward her, and she felt drawn to respond positively. Could it be that this fine young man with a burden like hers for China would be the special one God had for her?

The more she got to know him, the more she felt this a real possibility. She was growing in appreciation of both him and the idea, but the timing of an engagement seemed inappropriate. She was now in her final year of schooling at Moody and had applied to the China Inland Mission. Within months she would be accepted by the mission and on her way to China. John still had another year to go, and even if he applied to CIM, his acceptance would not necessarily be automatic. The two conferred with the Pages and were encouraged to keep their relationship warm while waiting to see how God might unfold their future.

Betty graduated from Moody in April 1931, having excelled academically all three years. The dean's assessment of her shows the high regard the school administration had of her:

A quiet, earnest sweet spirit. Limited perhaps by a certain self-consciousness. Dependable and faithful to tasks assigned her, yet not forceful. A soft voice. Always dressed simply but in good taste. Kind and gentle. Works well with others. Gifted as a writer of poetry. Has unique and original ideas. Daughter of missionaries.   —E.G. J.[4]

She went on to Philadelphia, attended the CIM candidate school, and was accepted as a missionary three months later. On her way to the West Coast to catch a ship to China, she was able to spend two glorious days in Chicago with John. They talked seriously about their future together but because of uncertainties decided best not to officially become engaged. Betty proceeded on to the West Coast, where she met up with four other young women appointees. They embarked for China on October 15, 1931.

Upon arrival in China, Betty was sent to Fowyang, a mission station in the northern part of Anhwei province. She was delighted to find that even after years of absence she could recall much of the language that she had learned as a child. After several months she and the other single women were suddenly evacuated because of Communist guerrilla activity. Another missionary in the area had been kidnapped by the guerrillas and never heard from again.

Since Betty's parents were returning to China from furlough, she took this opportunity to go to Shanghai to meet them. They had a joyous reunion, quickly catching up on one anothers' news. However, Betty did not realize that John would be on the next ship from the States. As she prepared to return to her inland station, she was suddenly stricken with a severe case of tonsillitis. This condition kept her in Shanghai for several additional weeks, just long enough for the arrival of the *Empress of Japan* with John on board. During the past year there had been missing letters coupled with a mix-up of her address, so that when the two finally met again, neither knew for sure where their relationship stood. Once explanations were made and desires revealed, they knew without question that they were meant to be together as husband and wife. John proposed, Betty accepted, and the two were formally engaged, to the delight of those who knew them.

Their week together passed quickly. Betty was reassigned to Fowyang and with a sad good-bye was on her way with a senior missionary couple. With a working knowledge of the local dialect, Betty plunged right back into the work. She loved the children, especially the girls. But the work was precarious to a degree with incidents of intrusions by soldiers that harassed the missionaries. When these unsettling events occurred, she would write the details to John, who was now in language school. Naturally John felt concerned for her safety, but learned to entrust his beloved to the hands of God.

Finally after a year apart the time for their wedding arrived. Betty returned to the home of her parents in Tsinan, awaiting John's arrival. The wedding took place in a colorful outdoor garden ceremony on a cool but clear October day. It was a typical Western wedding, filmed and still preserved today.[5] After the wedding meal the new couple went off on their honeymoon to Tsingtao, the place where Betty had lived as a child.

Blessed and full were the first days and months of marriage. Betty became pregnant, and in September 1934 she gave birth to a baby girl, naming her Helen Priscilla. After the baby's birth the Stams were asked by the mission to move to Tsingteh to take up the work there, under the condition that it was deemed safe to do so. John was quite cautious, carefully inquiring about the state of affairs in that region. The couple came to the conclusion that it was safe to begin the work there. They reached the city at the end of November. Betty busied herself with setting up house as John initiated ministry contacts.

When they were taken captive by two thousand Communists a few weeks later, Betty not only had concern for John's and her safety, but even more so for baby Helen's. Whatever her fate was to be, she did not want to see her precious baby harmed. As they were force-marched from Tsingteh, John walked next to her as a bound prisoner while she cuddled Helen on horseback in the cold for a full day.

It was the hand of Providence that kept Helen alive. Along the way their captors vacillated back and forth whether they should just kill the baby since she was considered a nuisance and a liability. At one point just as they were about to kill Helen, an old farmer came forward and pleaded for her life. "Then it's your life for hers!" was the angry retort. "I am willing to die," replied the farmer. He was executed then and there, saving the life of Helen.[6] Betty was quite shaken by the experience of coming within a hair's breadth of losing her baby and witnessing the sacrifice of the farmer. It caused her to wonder what else lay ahead. Would she lose her life? Would she live but lose her daughter? Would they all be killed, or would they all miraculously be spared? She did not know the answer as they were confined overnight to a small room in the town of Miaosheo.

The following morning the Communists entered the room where the Stams were imprisoned and gruffly forced Betty and John to prepare for execution. With a mother's sinking heart, she laid her baby down for the final time. Trembling, she wondered whatever would become of her. Reluctantly she turned away to follow the soldiers, entrusting Helen to the protection of her God. Recalling the vow she had made long ago in a far distant place, "All the people whom I love are to take a second place in my heart. . . . Work out Thy whole will in my life, at any cost, now and forever. To me to live is Christ. Amen." She prepared for the inevitable.

On a small hill outside the town, Betty momentarily trembled as she witnessed John's execution. The awful sight of her decapitated husband must have shocked her, but not enough to cause her to lose her resolve to follow to the very end. Only a martyr's grace could help her to do what she did next. With shaking hands and a trembling heart, she regained her composure and obediently knelt. A swift blow of the sword ushered her into God's and John's presence.

Just prior to their deaths, China missionary E. H. Hamilton wrote a martyr's poem to commemorate the recent martyrdom of one of his colleagues. The poem was widely circulated when the deaths of John and Betty became known, encouraging many to not lose heart.

Afraid? Of What?
To feel the spirit's glad release?
To pass from pain to perfect peace,
The strife and strain of life to cease?
Afraid—of that?

Afraid? Of What?
Afraid to see the Savior's face,
To hear His welcome, and to trace
The glory gleam from wounds of grace?
Afraid—of that?

Afraid? Of What?
A flash, a crash, a pierced heart;
Darkness, light, O Heaven's art!
A wound of His a counterpart!
Afraid—of that?

Afraid? Of What?
To do by death what life could not—
Baptize with blood a stony plot,
Till souls shall blossom from the spot?
Afraid—of that?[7]

1. Kathleen White, *John and Betty Stam*, 118.

2. Mrs. Howard Taylor, *The Triumph of John and Betty Stam*, 24–25.

3. Ibid., 27–28.

4. Moody Bible Institute Academic Records, Betty Stam.

5. Video footage of the wedding can be viewed in the mission archives at the Billy Graham Center, Wheaton, Illinois.

6. Mrs. Howard Taylor, *John and Betty Stam: A Story of Triumph*, 104.

7. James and Marti Hefley, *By Their Blood*, 57.

Born: October 31, 1896, Kingchow, Kansai, China

Nationality: American

Attended Moody: 1919

Country of Service: China

Mission: Evangelical Covenant Church

Ministry: Christian educator

Martyrdom: 1948, age 51, Hupeh province

Esther Victoria Nordlund

"The mission work is dear to my heart"

Esther Nordlund never shied away from the challenge of change. She learned early in ministry that circumstances can change very quickly. She also learned that if she was to be fully used by God she would need to be adaptable in a volatile world that was having an impact on an unsettled East Asia where she lived. Two world wars, amidst a period of continual political and social upheaval in China, would dog her ministry until the day she died. And before she did, she flexed and transitioned within that unpredictable world, maximizing her ministry efforts.

Early Years

Esther was born in 1896 to missionary parents in China. The first of five children, she grew up in Shaanxi province enmeshed in the life and culture of the ancient capital of China, Xi'an. Growing up, she became fluent in Chinese and as a thirteen-year-old demonstrated her commitment to Christ by baptism. When her parents went on furlough to the States in 1910, she experienced America for the first time. The family spent their time in northeastern Ohio connecting with her parents' family and home church. When it was time for their return to China, Esther and two siblings remained in the States. Staying behind in Ohio as a teenager rather than returning to her "homeland" China was the first change to which Esther learned to adjust.

Schooling

Although physically present in America, her heart and soul remained in China. She made it her singular goal to prepare herself for returning to the country she felt most a part of. After finishing high school in Youngstown, Ohio, in 1914, she enrolled at North Park College in Chicago. While there Esther increasingly felt she should prepare herself specifically to be an educator when she returned to China. After graduating from North Park in 1917, she went on to Wheaton College to earn a teaching certificate. Afterward, while awaiting appointment by the Evangelical Covenant church's mission board, she rounded out her education by briefly studying at Moody Bible Institute to receive Bible training.

Return to China

Esther was then appointed as a missionary to China with the Evangelical Covenant Church in 1920. That same year she, together with eight others in a band of new Covenant missionaries, sailed to China. Upon arrival, Esther had an advantage over the others by already being fluent in the Mandarin language. She began her teaching career at a time of great educational need, as 80 percent of China's population was illiterate. Additionally, the prevailing view that women were inferior and thus not worthy of education limited women to doing what they had been doing for centuries—tending fields and home. But Esther was a woman of change, and she knew that Chinese women wanted more out of life than that. So in the midst of skepticism and ridicule she took upon herself the role of teaching women. She spent the next six years doing just that.

As she did, political unrest, along with threats against missionaries, became increasingly pronounced. Fearful of the repeat of the 1900 Boxer mania, most foreign consulates advised their citizens to leave the country, precipitating a general evacuation of most missionaries. Faced with circumstances beyond her control, Esther returned to the States in 1926.

Alaska

After a year visiting family and churches, Esther knew that continued political unrest in China would prevent her from returning anytime soon. Not wanting to idly wait for the situation in China to clear up, she simply volunteered for the Covenant work in Alaska. She spent the next two years teaching native peoples in the isolated area of Unalakleet. She figured that what she could not do at the place of her first choice of service she could do in another. As it turned out, she was right. Her two years of teaching this people group were greatly valued.

Kidnapped!

By 1929 political unrest in China had subsided to the point that Esther was told by the mission it was safe for her to return. A few months later Esther did so, joined by her younger sister Mildred, a medical doctor. Esther threw herself back into the work, again taking up the education of Chinese women as her main focus. Ever aware of the danger that loomed around their compound in Hupeh, the missionaries guardedly continued their work. Esther had only been back in the country for a few months when one day without warning she, along with two other missionaries and a Chinese doctor, were suddenly kidnapped. Communist rebels held the four for ransom for a week. Providentially, they were eventually released unharmed through the intercession of the captive Chinese doctor.

As frightening as that experience was, after that incident Esther resolved all the more to continue her mission. She moved to the nearby city of Kingchow, where she taught English and music at a local school and also at Kingchow Theological Seminary. Esther was asked by the mission to move again, this time to the city of Fancheng.

Always willing to transition, she took up the new assignment. During her time there she demonstrated her love and concern for the people by throwing herself into the rescue and relief effort following the great Han River flood. She continued to labor in the midst of chaotic conditions until 1937, when the start of the Sino-Japanese War forced her out of China and back to the States. Another world event beyond her control—another uprooting and change.

The Philippines

While in the States, Esther had no choice but to wait out the war. She made herself useful by spending two years working in the Youngstown Covenant Church. During that time she revealed her deep-hearted concern for the Chinese people in a letter she wrote to T. W. Anderson, president of the Covenant church:

> The mission work is dear to my heart. I have had many opportunities to lead souls to Christ. I have also had opportunities to teach God's Word to school children and women. . . . My desire and wish is to continue in that work. God has led marvelously out there, and I have felt His presence while here at home on furlough with renewed strength and spiritual blessings. "The harvest is great but the laborers are few."[1]

While waiting for the war to end, she continually hoped for a chance to somehow get back to East Asia. Finally the opportunity came with the offer of a teaching position in the Philippines. Again, not afraid of change and a new challenge, in 1939 Esther flew to Manila and then on to Baguio in northern Luzon. There she established a Chinese language school for missionaries who were also stranded by the war. But her sights were ever on China, and after two years she made a bold move. First she flew to Hong Kong and then on to Szechwan province, then eventually made her way to Hupeh, just sixty-five miles from the battlefront. Once there she took charge of the Covenant church's educational work, women's ministry, and war relief efforts until taking furlough in 1945 as World War II came to an end.

Shot!

In May of 1947 Esther returned to China and was appointed as superintendent for the Covenant church of the Nanchang district. Sporadic incidents by the communists flared up in the area surrounding Hankow where Esther, along with several other missionaries, ministered. Undeterred, Esther continued her work.

Then in January of 1948, Esther, along with coworkers Dr. Alexis Berg and Martha Anderson, boarded a transit truck to attend mission council meetings in the neighboring town of Kingchow. Because of bandits roaming the area, the bus carried a contingent of armed guards. Early in the afternoon as the bus was making its way through the deserted hill country, a band of about fifty Communist bandits converged on the truck, forcing it to halt. The guards, seeing they were outnumbered, quickly abandoned the bus and passengers and fled. The unprotected passengers were then ordered off the bus and systematically robbed of their valuables. Even though it was cold, the three missionaries were forced to give up their coats and shoes. Dr. Berg asked that he might keep his passport and was promptly slapped and cursed for making such a request. After ransacking the bus, the bandits took off with their loot.

As they were leaving, however, four of them turned and surrounded the missionaries. The leader asked the others, "Shall we kill these foreigners?" He turned to Dr. Berg and asked if they were Americans. Dr. Berg (a Finn) did not reply. The leader then added, "Americans are the worst of all. They have done China much harm." He then drew his pistol and shot Dr. Berg at point-blank range through the head. When the shot was fired, Martha broke into sobs. The bandit, noticing her reaction, said she must be a relative and shot her too. One eyewitness later said that some of the passengers went to their knees and pleaded with the bandits to stop the killing. The bandits took a moment to discuss it among themselves, but then decided they should kill Esther also. Esther's last words were, "Yes, you may kill me too." Without hesitation, she too was shot through the head, falling dead next to the other two. The killers then went on their way.[2]

Leaving the bodies of the slain missionaries at the side of the road, the bus of shaken Chinese proceeded on to the next town and reported what had happened. Later that day the bodies of the three were recovered and taken to Kingchow. There the grief-stricken colleagues who had been awaiting their arrival instead prepared their slain friends for burial. Their coffins were taken back to Hankow for interment at the international cemetery.

The versatile Esther Nordlund who had adapted and changed her entire life had made her final transition.

Shut Down by Communists

Politically, a major transition was taking place in China too. The deaths of Esther and her colleagues triggered a chain of events that brought fifty years of work by the Covenant church in China to an abrupt end. Shortly after that tragic event, the remaining Covenant missionaries were evacuated. A new era of Communist rule now prevailed, shutting the door to all mission work from the outside for decades to come.

1. Liang Kazu Wu, "The Lives and Martyrdom of China Missionaries Esther V. Nordlund, Martha J. Anderson, and Alexis F. Berg," 15–16.
2. Russell A. Cervin, *Covenant Missions in China/Taiwan*, 16.

AFRICA

Born: January 30, 1866, Willshire, Ohio

Nationality: American

Attended Moody: 1895–1896

Country of Service: Sierra Leone

Mission: United Brethren

Ministry: Teacher

Martyrdom: 1898, age 32, Rotufunk

Ella Mary Schenck

"That which our lives cannot do, our deaths may do"

The small band of United Brethren in Christ missionaries that sailed out of New York harbor on October 1, 1897, was full of anticipation of what lay ahead. The five missionaries had no illusions about what to expect as they headed for Africa, since most had already spent a term of service in Sierra Leone. West Africa had the dubious distinction of being known as "the white man's grave," and some of their colleagues already lay buried in its soil.

Four days out of port as Ella sat in her cabin pondering her future, she wrote to her good friend and former coworker Lida West. Lida's husband had died in Sierra Leone during the past term, and now Lida remained in the States. In her letter Ella mentioned that she would honor the memory of Lida's husband by visiting his grave upon her arrival in Africa. Then in quiet confidence Ella emptied her heart to her friend: "I am in many respects glad to go back; more happy than when I first went, but the home-leaving was harder than before. However, I am trusting my Lord, as I believe He is going just before me and choosing the way, and I am glad in Him. I have a deep abiding peace and comfort, which makes and keeps me strong. I know you'll pray hard that much of the Master's will may be wrought in me."[1]

Many missionaries had paid the ultimate price in West Africa—their lives taken by strange sicknesses and disease. But very few had had their lives snatched away as a result of violent action on the part of the people they went to serve; they generally felt safe in that regard. But the tranquility aboard ship gave no hint to what lay ahead.

Unbeknown to Ella and her group, exactly seven months to the day that they pulled away from America's shore, they would experience a bloodbath of violence and horror that would snuff out their lives.

The British Oppression

As the ship was making for England and then on to Western Africa, trouble was brewing in Sierra Leone. The British had declared the country a protectorate a year earlier. They had divided the land into five districts. The British district commissioner, who was vested with power to administer the land, made changes in the traditional system of government and was given full judicial rights. Consequently, local tribal chiefs and kings were filled with consternation by the curbing of their own right to rule.

Then the oppression of the British went a step further. They greedily declared it their right to exploit all mineral and natural resources for themselves. They further exacerbated the situation by imposing a tax on the very huts in which the people lived. Cruelly subjugated and woefully exploited, the people looked for a deliverer who would rise up and lead them in a movement to throw off this foreign yoke.

Native Uprising

The daring chief of the Kasseh tribe, Bai Bureh, was just that man. At the same time that Ella and the other missionaries reached Freetown, the capital of Sierra Leone, Bai Bureh began his counter-colonial action. By mid-February the group of missionaries had made their way by boat to their remote inland station at Rotufunk on the Bumpe River. Meanwhile, Bai Bureh had declared open revolt against the British. People across the entire countryside from Karena to Port Loko, infuriated by the demands of the foreign oppressor, supported Bai Bureh's resistance movement. The bloody struggle that ensued became known as the Hut Tax War.

Bai Bureh's warriors began cutting British communication lines and attacking all aliens, whether British or Creole. By late April they had destroyed much British and Creole property and had slaughtered hundreds of people. Encouraged by the success of Bai Bureh, the movement gained an even stronger following. Many natives were now on a rampage throughout the country, indiscriminately killing and burning anything foreign.

By the end of April word reached the missionaries at Rotufunk that the rebels were within reach of them. This flourishing United Brethren mission was staffed with six Americans: Reverend and Mrs. Isaac Cain, Reverend Arthur Ward, medical doctors Marietta Hatfield and Mary Archer, and Ella. The Americans felt that they had little to fear. After all, they were not British, and during the previous wars of the 1870s and 1880s Americans were left unmolested.

Attempted Escape

However, on May 1, with the war advancing ever closer, they realized they were in grave danger. Word reached them that farther upriver some other American missionaries had been killed. Sympathetic natives told them that they were the next target of the rebels' wrath. Alarmed, they decided to evacuate the station and make their way to Freeport. However, some days earlier Arthur Ward had taken the mission boat to Freeport on routine business, leaving the others no means of escape. Their only hope was to attempt to escape on foot across the rugged terrain, something they had never done before.

Ella and her colleagues set out on the trail, but shortly after getting under way their worst fears were realized. The party was discovered and quickly surrounded by sword-wielding warriors. Their escape had been foiled barely before it could begin. Ella's hands were bound behind her back, and she and the others were forcibly marched back into Rotufunk. By the wild look on the warriors' faces and roughness of their treatment, she must have considered that unless God intervened on their behalf, this would be her end.

Ohio Upbringing

Ella had been born near Willshire, Ohio, on January 30, 1866. Nine months earlier the Civil War had come to an end, and the country was settling back into normalcy. Her father, Reverend D. J. Schenck, was a pastor in the United Brethren in Christ Church of the Auglaize Conference. When Ella was only four years old, her mother died. A few years later her father married a woman who lovingly raised Ella. At the age of thirteen she was converted and became a member in the United Brethren in Christ Church (U.B.C.).

After high school Ella enrolled at Eastern Indiana Normal College. She was a bright student, graduating from the teacher's course in a shorter time than any in her class. She studied primary education and stenography and also became knowledgeable in photography. She took a job as a schoolteacher and seemed destined to a typical American middle-class way of life. But then the Lord began to speak to her as she heard stories of the mission work of the U.B.C. in Africa. Feeling compelled by God to utilize her skill as a teacher, one day she approached her father and asked, "Would you consent to my going to Africa?" Scarcely weighing her question, he answered, "Yes, you may go." Cheerfully she replied, "Well, then I am going."[2]

First Term in Africa

Shortly afterward she applied to and was accepted by the foreign mission board of the U.B.C. Beginning in 1875, the sending out of single women through the newly organized Women's Missionary Association had augmented the denomination's mission. Ella, being single, was sent out through this arm of the church. In the company of several other U.B.C. missionaries, on September 23, 1891, at the age of twenty-five, Ella sailed from New York on the *S.S. City of Chicago* for West Africa.

The party arrived at Freetown two months later. Upon arrival, Ella discovered she had much to learn. With no cultural training and little resistance to the tropical heat, she felt out of place. But over time she began to do more than just survive. She found that she did have a place as a matron in the girls' school at the interior station of Rotufunk. Here she became a model teacher to native young girls. Besides this assignment, she also took delight in direct work with the people in their homes. Ella had abilities as a public speaker too, and, it was said, "she was at home in the pulpit and a leader of Sunday morning seeker classes."[3]

After three years, the rigors of the tropics began to take a toll on her health, and she took a home leave. When she departed, a number of the children clung to her, begging her to return once again.

In the States

Arriving back in the Midwest, Ella made her home in Pleasant Mills, Indiana. Reflecting on her work in Africa, she felt the need for some Bible and evangelistic training. Knowing she could get this training at Moody Bible Institute, she enrolled in December. She finished her studies the following April, sensing that the classes and practical evangelistic work had prepared her for work again in Africa. She then took a position as a schoolteacher in Indiana for a year, while deciding whether she really should return to Sierra Leone or not. Finally, just like the first time, she felt divinely compelled to go.

On a warm summer evening in August of 1897 at the U.B.C. church of Decatur, Indiana, in the presence of her father, relatives, and friends, Ella knelt at the altar. She was consecrated by the

Conference for service back to Africa. Standing in front of her loved ones, it was said by one present that "she was joyous, exulting in Christ. . . . Her spirit and presence and power will live in memory always of that Conference."[4]

Now, just seven months later, she found herself with her hands bound together, being force-marched by frenzied rebels back to the place she and her colleagues had just fled.

The Massacre

The rebels brought their five prisoners to the center of the Rotufunk mission station in plain sight of all. There was no hiding the gruesome deeds they were about to perform. First they commanded Ella, along with the others, to disrobe. Next, they turned their weapons on their captives, mercilessly hacking them to death, as they stood defenseless. While this was happening, some of the men grabbed Ella, took her over to the barracks, and forced themselves on her, venting their lust. Once through, as she lay helpless and humiliated, they slashed her body with a cutlass, ending her life. Finally they turned their attention to the mission buildings—the church, school, barracks, and hospital—putting them ablaze until all burned to the ground. They then left, leaving behind the smoldering ruins of the compound with its mutilated bodies strewn around in pools of blood.

Back in Indiana, word reached Ella's loved ones of her cruel death. Reflecting back on her August commissioning by the Conference, Dr. J. W. Hott commented, "How can we but believe that the prayers of that Conference for her, that Jesus would be with her always, even to the end, were answered in that awful moment of her martyrdom, and that the Savior lifted her above all the torture and sweetly held her spirit in His keeping till the mortal agony was past."[5]

What "Death May Do"

During her first term in Sierra Leone, on the occasion of the death of two of her associates, Ella had written,

> I can think of nothing that would make death more welcomed than to meet it here, to die for these dear children as my Savior died for me. It is the suffering and dying Savior that melts the stony heart. So with us—that which our lives cannot do our deaths may do.[6]

Two years later the U.B.C. reopened the work at Rotufunk and rebuilt the station. Through the years that followed, a flourishing work again was realized, which also became the seed for five new mission stations. For Ella Mary Schenck, the first martyr of Moody, it may well be that what she could not do in life was done through her death.

1. *Women's Evangel*, 124.
2. Ibid., 123.
3. Ibid., 124.
4. Ibid., 119.
5. Ibid.
6. Ibid., 124.

Born: January 10, 1867, Indiana, Pennsylvania

Nationality: American

Attended Moody: 1907

Country of Service: Kenya

Mission: Africa Inland Mission

Ministry: Office administrator/women's ministry

Martyrdom: 1930, age 63, Kijabe

Hulda Jane Stumpf

"On bended knee and with heart bowed to God"

Hulda stood in her yard gazing across the breadth of one of the world's most beautiful expanses. The Great Rift Valley, which lay quietly below and around her, was full of nature's most exquisite beauty. The valley was plentiful with wildlife, and at times she could spot zebras, giraffes, elephants, and other animals. She stood pondering the immensity of this valley, stretching north as far as the Dead Sea in Palestine, then all the way to the country of Mozambique to the south. At the Dead Sea it was 1,300 feet below sea level. But here at the equator where she stood, it was more than a mile above that mark. At its start the valley was dry and very much "dead," but here it was fresh and alive with the scent of life and so many species of birds and animals that she could barely keep track of all she had seen during her twenty-two years of service at Kijabe.

As she stood gazing, her thoughts must have taken her back to her home in mountainous western Pennsylvania. She reminisced about the hills and the valleys that surrounded her as a child and young adult. That too was a beautiful setting that she once thought could not be matched. Now that she had experienced all that surrounded her in Kenya, she knew there was no comparison between the two. However, the outward beauty and tranquility of this vast valley belied the tension and turmoil that lay within. Indeed, although the environs portrayed a sense of the innocence of Eden, the people who lived within it did not.

Gospel and Culture

Wherever the gospel is newly preached, it contends with those practices in culture that stand contrary to God's moral law. In India it was the practice of suttee—the burning alive of the widow on her husband's funeral pyre. In China it was the practice of foot binding —intentionally keeping young girls' feet petite for the purpose of sexual attraction. In some areas of South America, the gruesome practice of human sacrifice was an issue. Across the continent of Africa, especially East Africa, it has been (and continues to be today) the issue of female circumcision. Little could Hulda have imagined, as she stood admiring the colorful African sunset across the valley, that the emotion of this issue would precipitate the taking of her life.

Throughout Christian history, missionaries have been martyred for any number of reasons. Some have been political reasons, others theological. Some have been martyred in the midst of rebellion, others because of greed. Some were martyred because of religious intolerance, others out of plain ignorance. However, the number who were martyred because of cultural tension within the church itself have been few. Hulda Stumpf was one of these few.

Pennsylvania Upbringing

Born in the town of Indiana, Pennsylvania, on January 10, 1867, Hulda was one of four children. Growing up, she attended the local Church of Christ as a moral, upright, yet nominal member. After high school she went on to attend a business college for six months and then New York Music School for two years after that. These two schools trained her for what she would later be known best for in her missionary service—an administrator and talented singer. Her next twenty years were rather uneventful, spent first as a clerk, then a stenographer, and finally as a teacher of shorthand at the Indiana Business College in her hometown.

Conversion and Training

In July of 1906, when she was thirty-nine, a vast change came over Hulda's life. For the first time she truly understood the gospel and her need for a personal conversion to Christ. She was completely transformed from being merely a good, moral church member to one whose every thought and desire was to glorify God. With a new outlook on life, she desired to serve God as far as her talents would allow. Hulda now felt led to serve God as a missionary, so she applied to the Africa Inland Mission (AIM). She gained the appointment with the provision that she would first receive some formal Bible training before going to Kenya.

Moody Bible Institute was the school of choice for Hulda. She entered in May of 1907. At forty years of age, she was one of the oldest students to that point to ever study at Moody. Two months later she finished the minimum required by AIM. The academic record simply says of her time at Moody that she was "direct, businesslike, and kind."[1] Those were the virtues that would characterize her life as a missionary as well.

The Quiet Missionary

Hulda reached Africa in late 1907. After a time of orientation, she was assigned to the AIM mission center at Kijabe, fifty miles north of Nairobi. Since she had proven skills in office management, Hulda was given the task of office secretary to the director of the Kijabe mission. In the quietness of a humble servant, she took on all the administrative tasks that were handed to her. For twenty-two years she worked, unheralded, facilitating the work of others.

However, all her time was not confined to the office. When opportunity allowed, she studied the culture and ways of the people. When time permitted, she took extended trips to isolated mission outposts in the interior so she could meet and better understand the living conditions of the missionaries who served there. Through the years she wrote numerous articles for the AIM journal *Inland Africa* on various aspects of African culture and the work being done among the people throughout the country. Although she herself was not what most viewed as a "remarkable" missionary, she wrote up the stories of others who were. Hulda was content to be behind the scenes, taking little of the credit.

The longer Hulda served as a missionary, the more she understood the importance of prayer and submission to God's will. On the occasion of her second return to Africa, she wrote in the mission journal,

> The message I would leave with you as I set forth a second time to bear His message again is the same as someone has said: "In like manner as David Livingston went out of Africa praying, so ought a man to enter." So on bended knee and with heart bowed to God in submission to His will, I bid you farewell.[2]

Opposition from Within

How little could Hulda have fathomed what submission to God's will would mean to her personally. As she continued to quietly go about her duties at the Kijabe office, unrest was brewing in the villages throughout the valley. All the missionaries were fully aware of the instability. The time-honored African custom of female circumcision was under attack in the churches. Many in the African church felt that this custom, also known as female genital mutilation (FGM), was important to maintain. They felt the church had no right either to interfere with or abolish its practice. Others, readily led by the missionaries, felt that it was harmful to the young teenage girls who underwent its cruel practice. Many young girls died, others were permanently maimed, and all were handicapped in the performance of natural relations because of it.

When the missionaries realized the Kenyan Christians were unable to resolve the issue themselves, they stepped in. First they tried to do the procedure at the mission hospital to curtail the unsanitary method performed in the villages. It was not long until the doctors and nurses could see no sense doing the procedure at all and refused to do so anymore.

Next they tried a health education program, showing the negative effects of the practice on society as a whole. But their efforts were to no avail. Finally, they used Scripture teaching to show the brutality and sinfulness of the practice. Some church leaders and people agreed it was wrong and pushed to ban the practice. Others did not agree and lobbied hard to retain it. Most men simply refused to marry an uncircumcised woman.

By late 1929, the issue had reached such heated debate that it caused much discord both within churches and without. Ninety percent of AIM's converts left the mission churches to begin their own ministries. There was not a village throughout the entire region where AIM worked that was not affected. Emotions were running high, and it was only a matter of time before the issue would explode in some ghastly demonstration. Hulda, who was spending more of her time working among the women, became a focal person in the cultural debate. This is probably what led to her death.

Death in the New Year

On the evening of January 1, 1930, all the missionaries of Kijabe station met together as usual for their Wednesday night prayer meeting.

Earlier in the day they had brought in the New Year in celebration, and now for a second time they were together and on their knees asking God to direct their work in the new year and new decade. Hulda, as usual, played the organ for the group. When the meeting was over, she said good night to everyone for what would turn out to be a final good-bye. She returned to her modest two-room cottage in which she had lived for many years.

When Hulda retired for the night, she could not have had the slightest hint of the terror that was about to befall her. After she fell asleep, a man entered her house undetected by breaking in a side window. Once in, he rushed to her bed and assaulted her before she knew what was happening. Hulda had little chance to defend herself against the intruder's youthful strength. He first sexually molested her and then with his bare hands choked her until she lay lifeless. Then, to make his point, he performed his appalling deed, mutilating her in a fashion and with an instrument that could leave no doubt that it was the work of a circumcision fanatic. His deed completed, he left the same way he had entered, without lifting a thing from her house.[3]

Hulda's body was discovered by her houseboy early the following morning. The mission leader and doctor were immediately summoned. The message that was intended by her deranged killer became apparent to all. The heat of controversy over the matter of circumcision had climaxed in the taking of a missionary's life—Hulda's. Two days later her body was put to rest by fellow missionaries in that beautiful valley she had come to love and call home.

1. Moody Bible Institute Academic Records, Hulda Stumpf.
2. Hulda Stumpf, "Farewell Words," 14.
3. Various sources confirmed the gruesome manner of her death. Especially noteworthy is the telegram included in the letter by H.W.E. dated January 4, 1912.

Born: December 8, 1891, Kenosha, Wisconsin

Nationality: American

Graduated from Moody: 1915

Country of Service: Cameroon

Mission: United Presbyterian Board, USA

Ministry: Teacher, writer, hostess

Martyrdom: 1949, age 58, Elat

Lucia Hammond Cozzens

"The great privilege that is mine"

As I trek through the great jungle of Africa, I am thrilled with the great privilege that is mine. The path is an inconspicuous line, flanked by majestic trees and dense undergrowth, with here and there wonderfully delicate flowers in those parts of the forest whose beauty is yet only slightly damaged by the encroachment of an embryo civilization. It is cool and fresh now in the early morning. I am wearing a khaki coat, with coppers and safety pins, pencil and paper in its pockets. Two safety pins have just been bartered for a hand of bananas for my porters. The pencil and paper are being used to jot down these lines to you as I go along in my chair, hearing only the birds and the tread of my porters' feet.[1]

So began Lucia's account of one of her many treks into the jungle of Cameroon. But visiting surrounding tribal peoples was not actually her main mission responsibility. Rather, she spent most of her time as a teacher, writer, hostess, and editor of mission articles.

Lucia was rather ordinary. She looked ordinary and had an ordinary upbringing and an ordinary education. Nothing extraordinary about her person or her work commends her to mission history except that in her murder she was declared a martyr. Even the circumstance surrounding her death was rather ordinary.

Pre-field Years

Lucia was born in Kenosha, Wisconsin, in December 1891. Born in a Christian home, she believed in Christ early and determined to be a missionary from a young age. Following high school, she attended a business college and then proved herself a savvy businesswoman for five years. However, she was not satisfied with business, and acting upon the call of God in her life for missionary work, she decided to resign her job.

Lucia enrolled in the Bible-Music course at Moody Bible Institute in January 1914. She was not a standout student, but rather seen as steady and reliable. In fact, she was an ordinary student who earned average grades. Socially, she kept her distance from others to the point it was said that she " . . . needs the softening and understanding that comes to one through general social relationships."[2] However, what Lucia lacked in academic and social acumen she made up in performance in ministry. She excelled while working at a city mission. She completed the Moody course after two years and then graduated.

Lucia moved to Muncie, Indiana, where she worked three years as a secretary for the local Y.W.C.A. She was waiting out the world war that prevented new missionary volunteers like her from traveling overseas.

Before leaving Chicago for Muncie, Lucia had applied to what was then called The Board of Foreign Missions of The Presbyterian Church in the U.S.A. After getting settled in Muncie, Lucia joined the First Presbyterian Church, since that was the denomination with which she was going to serve. The board appointed her a missionary in December 1918 and assigned her to West Africa early the next year.

Ministry in Cameroon

In September of 1919 on the heels of World War I, as a mature twenty-seven-year-old, Lucia arrived in France for language study. French was becoming the primary language of most of Cameroon, since it had become a French-mandated territory following World War I.

Ten months later she arrived in Cameroon. No sooner had she

arrived then she met another single American missionary who took a quick interest in her. Edwin Cozzens, who had spent the previous five years there, wooed Lucia into a courtship. As the associate director of the Frank James Industrial School at Elat, he was eager to have Lucia as his wife. Lucia was eager to oblige. Within eighteen months (half of the mission's mandated waiting time) they were married. Although they did not have children, their marriage was enduring.

Lucia was not strong in health, but was determined in spirit to do what needed to be done around the station and the school. She was able to accomplish an enormous amount of work by pacing herself through a rigid routine. She took over the responsibility of the Community House for wives and children, taught Bible, hygiene, and sewing, and she learned the Bulu language. She set up a hospitality house for traveling missionaries and diplomats, for which she became known over much of West Africa. She also had oversight of the bookstore and school library.

Probably her lasting and greatest accomplishment was in the field of literature. Lucia edited and contributed for years to the mission's quarterly magazine, *The Drum Call*. Her thoughts, recipes, travelogues, and cultural observations are preserved in issue after issue of this publication. The monthly newsletter, *Mefoe*, in the vernacular language, was also her work. Additionally, she wrote a book and a commentary on Romans in the Bulu language. Lucia's work was valuable to the overall work of the mission. After twenty-five years of service she would write:

> We have seen that every quality, every talent a person may possess is utilized if one is a missionary. Do you wish to discover and use all your latent abilities? Be a missionary! And if you are a missionary sooner or later there will be revealed to you—and alas to others!—the innate flaws and weaknesses of your

nature, as well as unexpected talents. Being a missionary wrings out of you the last drop of good and bad there is within you.[3]

A Sudden Death

And then the unexpected happened. In October of 1949 her husband, Edwin, was on mission business to neighboring Guinea and had left Lucia home alone. Before dawn one morning an intruder sneaked into the Cozzens's home and surprised Lucia while she was still in bed. Startled from her sleep, she didn't have time to defend herself. The murderer jumped at her and stabbed her repeatedly until she was dead. He fled the house, leaving no clues as to what motivated the dastardly action.

Lucia was buried the following day at Elat. African believers, French officials, and the missions community came to pay their respects to one they had grown to admire and respect. The ranking French district office spoke the following tribute:

> In the name of the High-Commissioner of the Cameroon, in the name of the Administration of the N'Tem and finally in my own name, I have the sad task of coming to pay my respects for the last time to Mrs. Cozzens. After 29 years of devotion and love, it was necessary that as a final act of this long period of self-sacrifice she pour out her blood on the soil of this country. May this generous blood bring forth an abundant increase of faith, of love and of devotion. May this blood wash the sins and the follies of the people of the N'Tem. I am certain that in the generosity of her heart, Mrs. Cozzens has forgiven the one who raised his hand against her. . . . To Mr. Cozzens, who loses his admirable life-companion, we would express our deep sympathy and our affection in this trial that

has befallen him. With him we fellowship in the sorrow of the memory which remains to us of a life entirely consecrated to radiating good around her.[4]

Edwin returned home a few days later to discover an empty house and a fresh grave. The voice that cheered him along in ministry for years was now silent. Her presence was gone. What's more, the perpetrator of this seemingly senseless act was never discovered.

Exemption from His "Go"?

But even after her death, Lucia spoke from the grave. The same month of her death her latest article appeared in the October issue of *The Drum Call.* In it she challenged believers to remember their personal responsibility to the cause of Christ, writing:

> "Go, therefore and make disciples of all nations" . . . The Lord commands us saying, I have sent you to be a light . . . that you may bring salvation to the uttermost parts of the earth. As Dr. Speer observed so many years ago, how can we claim for ourselves Christ's "Come unto me" and claim exemption from his "Go"?[5]

Lucia took seriously Christ's command to go. She spent her life as an unheralded, ordinary missionary doing ordinary mission things, which, paradoxically, when all woven together make the work of missions so extraordinary.

1. Lucia Cozzens, "Day by Day on a Trekking Trip," October 8, 1927, 1.
2. Moody Bible Institute Academic Records, Lucia Hammond.
3. Lucia Cozzens, "What Are You Doing?" in *The Drum Call,* October, 1949, 21.
4. Memorial Minutes on Mrs. Edwin Cozzens, Nov. 14, 15, 1949, 2.
5. Cozzens, "What Are You Doing?", 23.

Born: April 9, 1914, Richmond, Virginia

Nationality: American

Graduated from Moody: 1945

Country of Service: Congo

Mission: Unevangelized Fields Mission

Ministry: Bible teaching/evangelism

Martyrdom: 1964, age 50, Banalia

Mary Elizabeth Baker

"With me it was settled long ago."

Simba is the Swahili word for "lion." It was the name rebel forces took for themselves in the Congo against the government in the mid-1960s. It was also the name that Mary Baker uncannily gave to her loyal dog years before. Unknowingly, she had given to her "best friend" the same name of those who would one day take her life.

For almost twenty years Mary had been working in the Congo doing Bible teaching and general evangelistic work. She lived right among the people in a little village, Bopepe, sharing in their joys and sorrows, hopes and fears. She literally became one with the people, adjusting to their culture and way of life in a way that it became her very own. Over time villagers were evangelized and discipled, a church was established, and a clinic was erected. A nurse from England joined her.

Mary looked younger than her age of fifty. She was the happy-go-lucky incurable optimist who saw the positive side of every situation. A great talker from Virginia, she loved sharing a cup of tea with whoever happened to be around. She loved the Congolese, and they loved her in return. She proved her loyalty to them during a crisis in 1960 when most missionaries abandoned their stations while she stayed. The people never forgot that, and in return they stayed loyal to her until the day of her death.[1]

Before the Congo

Mary was born in Richmond, Virginia, in 1914. She wanted to pave a way for herself, and after high school competently held a variety of jobs as a bookkeeper and stenographer. She eventually became a senior clerk for the State Auditor of Public Accounts for the Commonwealth of

Virginia. Although she was not a believer at the time, Mary was doing very well for herself.

Then God got ahold of her life, and at the age of twenty-five, she gladly gave herself over to Him.

Feeling called by God to serve full-time as a missionary, she entered Moody in 1943 to prepare for that very thing. Two and a half years later she graduated from the missionary program just as World War II was coming to an end. With the war over and a missions degree fresh in hand, she was accepted by Unevangelized Fields Mission (later renamed UFM, and now CrossWorld). Not long afterwards, she was on her way to the Congo.

Mary arrived in the Congo in 1946 at the age of thirty-two. The interior village of Bopepe asked for a missionary, so that is where she went. She would spend the rest of her life there. Over the next eighteen years she became such an integral part of the village that they gave her her own "drum name." The Congolese still used the drum as a means of communication. She was given the name "Emi Wnagai Kegel Manbulu." The syllables for her name could be reproduced on the drum, enabling her to be contacted by this traditional jungle telegraph.

The Simba Crisis

The Simba revolt erupted in earnest in mid-1964. In August of that year, Mary's coworker, Margaret Hayes, left her alone at Bopepe while she took a much-deserved break from the work. Being alone was of little concern to Mary, as she had worked alone many times before. However, this time was different. The local pastor had warned both the foreign missionaries and local Christians that Simba danger loomed near. He prophetically foresaw that unless intervention came from the government, there could well be a bloodbath in the area within weeks. How true was his prediction. As a single missionary on her own Mary took courage in Psalm 54:

> Save me, O God, by thy name, and judge me by thy strength.
> Hear my prayer, O God; give ear to the words of my mouth.
> —Psalm 54:1–2, KJV

Early one afternoon as Mary was resting, a carload of eight Simba men stopped nearby and sneaked up on her house. Banging on her door, they demanded to be let in to search it. Once inside, they grabbed her and verbally berated her, but stopped short of molesting her. Frustrated at her calmness, they forced her out on the veranda. Putting a gun to her head, they asked if she wanted to die. She calmly told them she wasn't afraid and was quite ready to die. Admiring her courage, they put the gun down. Lifting her house of valuable items, including her two-way mission radio, they left. The villagers who witnessed the incident admired her for her courage, saying, "Truly she practices what she preaches."[2]

> For strangers are risen up against me, and oppressors seek after my soul: they have not set God before them. Selah.
> —Psalm 54:3, KJV

About a week later her coworker Margaret was able by sheer determination to return to Bopepe over the dangerous roads that were now patrolled by the Simbas. Mary and the villagers were at the church as the jeep carrying Margaret entered the mission compound. Seeing Margaret, Mary ran from the service crying as she embraced her friend. She warned her that the Simbas were still in and around the village. The Simbas informed the two that, although they did not believe in what they taught, they could continue their work under their watchful eye.

Whenever the Simbas were in need of anything, they would show up at the women's house and take whatever they pleased. By the end of September, they had just about depleted the food and fuel supply of the two women. Mary and Margaret were forced to go on emergency rations, supplementing their meager diet by what they could glean from the gardens.

Meanwhile the Simbas continued to harass them. Often trucks packed with Simbas would drive past, singing songs of hate. Representatives of the M.N.C., the rebel political party, would rudely enter their home and demand that the women purchase political party cards. They would bring their wounded to the clinic, sometimes at 3:00 in the morning, and demand they be treated. One Sunday as the two missionaries were worshiping in the church, a truck filled with Simbas stopped, and the men barged into the service. They looked around menacingly and demanded the white women treat one of their ailing comrades. Once outside, Mary and Margaret cringed as the air erupted with gunfire as one of the Simbas empted his rifle into a nearby tree. This in turn emptied the church of its frightened parishioners.[3]

Captive of the Simbas

> Behold, God is mine helper: the Lord is with them that uphold my soul. —Psalm 54:4, KJV

Toward the end of October, a mysterious plane flew over the village at night. Rumors began to circulate that the white people— either missionaries or plantation owners—were clandestinely calling

the planes. This prompted the rebels to dispatch trucks to the out-
lying areas to collect all foreigners. Two nights later a truck rolled into
Bopepe and pulled up to the women's house. Mary went out to find
spear-carrying rebels on the veranda. Their bodies were decorated
with palm leaves and rubbed with "magical" medicine. Rudely push-
ing her inside, they informed her that she and Margaret were under
arrest.

As morning broke the women were told by the Simbas that they
were to go with them to the town of Banalia, where they were to be
permanently held. Since no trucks were available for transport, they
were forced to make the trip on foot. As Mary and Margaret began
walking out of the village, the people lined the road, openly crying
and mourning. Many took their hands and whispered, "God go with
you." Some of them angrily taunted the Simbas, smacking and verbally assaulting them for forcing their "Mamas" away like that. The
two found renewed strength by this show of support.

The fifteen-mile trek to Banalia was especially challenging for
Mary. Every two or three miles she needed to stop for rest. Her feet
became sore and blistered as the tropical heat sapped her strength.
The rebels were sympathetic enough to allow rest and drinks along
the way, but kept their captives moving. By nightfall the exhausted
party reached their destination. Upon seeing Mary and Margaret, the
commander of the base was actually sympathetic toward them, apolo-
gizing for the treatment they were receiving. He even read to them the
orders sent from Stanleyville (the capital) that justified his actions.[4]

The two were taken to a building that had recently been ran-
sacked. They discovered it was filthy, lacking water, and devoid of
furniture. In this prison-house Mary was to spend the last weeks of
her life. But not all was doom and gloom. Other missionaries had
been rounded up as well and were trickling into the increasingly
crowded house. Two other missionary couples, another single lady,

and three Catholic nuns became part of the new captive community. Together, they would encourage one another through their ordeal.

> He shall reward evil unto mine enemies: cut them off in thy
> truth.   —Psalm 54:5, KJV

Over the next three weeks, as their rebel cause became more desperate, the rebels became increasingly hostile toward their captives. The rebellion was not going well, and they were being driven back and sustaining numerous casualties. Sensing she would never be freed, Mary prepared herself for death. She told Margaret outright on three occasions that she was not going to survive and that she was at peace dying there in Banalia, close to her people.

Then surprisingly, on November 23, Mary was delighted to hear that Margaret was being released to return to Bopepe because her nursing expertise was sorely needed there. The others were informed that they too would soon be released. As Margaret turned to leave, she promised Mary she would get the place in order and send a bicycle so she wouldn't have to make the trip back on foot. An air of optimism prevailed, as the missionaries hoped that the crisis would soon be over.

However, their good fortune was quickly reversed due to events happening farther to the south. On that same November night, an international force of paratroopers dropped into Stanleyville, the capital city, to free twelve hundred expatriate hostages being held. In the fighting that ensued, most hostages were rescued. But over thirty-five of them, including Dr. Paul Carlson, the well-known and highly respected American medical missionary, lost their lives.

Less than a day later, the city and surrounding area were secured. The government, backed by the international community, was back in control.

The Banalia Massacre

I will freely sacrifice unto thee: I will praise thy name, O Lord;
for it is good. —Psalm 54:6, KJV

Routed, truckloads of Simbas frantically retreated from Stanleyville north to Banalia. Angry because of their losses caused by foreign intervention, they determined to take revenge on any remaining white hostages. Earlier that week the rebel leader, General Olenga, had broadcast to his followers that if there was an outside attack on Stanleyville, all white people were to be killed.

Just days earlier Mary had penned her final letter to her friends in Stanleyville, which said:

> The Word of God has become very precious these days—like the voice of the tender Shepherd speaking directly now in our need. You are all constantly in my heart, and we pray for you individually and together. I know that each of you has suffered—if not physically, there have been the mental strains in Stan that I'm sure have been terrific, and my little bouts with the whole situation have been very easy to bear comparatively; I only tell you of them that you might know how it has been. As I said to B.M. the other day, with me, it was settled long ago, "by life or by death" and there it rests! My special Psalm has been 54: read it![5]

It was midafternoon when the rebels swarmed into Banalia. Within an hour they had all the foreigners rounded up—Mary, the Sharpes with their three children, the Parrys with their two children, Ruby Gray, the three Catholic nuns, and a Dutch priest. Angrily, the

Simbas hustled their fifteen prisoners down to the river's ferry landing. Once there, they were lined up in a row and one by one called forward. Mercilessly each was either shot, hacked, or speared to death. Mary fell, and her body was tossed into the river along with the others. None were ever recovered.

> For he hath delivered me out of all trouble: and mine eye hath seen his desire upon mine enemies. —Psalm 54:7, KJV

Mary was not physically delivered from her troubles. Instead hers was a spiritual deliverance. Through it all, she was given a martyr's grace. She would never have considered the Simbas her enemies— only misguided Congolese who were searching for something better than what they had.

Resuming and Remembering

It was another year before the Simba rebellion was fully subdued. But when it was, peace was finally restored to the war-torn country. The work of missions was then able to resume. Rebuilding, restaffing, and remembering fallen colleagues took precedence at the start.

On December 5, 1965, just a little over a year after the Banalia massacre, a memorial program commemorating the death of Mary and her colleagues was held at the headquarters of UFM in Bala-Cynwyd, Pennsylvania. Mary's pastor from Virginia, Dr. Richard Seume, was the main speaker. A large plaque was unveiled, listing the names of the Congo martyrs. Mary's name tops the list. Those who pass through the doors of the mission cannot help but notice that plaque and be reminded of the high price of doing missions in a volatile world.

1. Margaret Hayes, *Captive of the Simbas*, 35–36

2. Ibid., 31

3. Ibid., 40–44.

4. Ibid., 50–53.

5. Mary Baker, personal letter, August 19, 1964, 3.

Born: September 14, 1949, La Paz, Bolivia

Nationality: Canadian

Graduated from Moody: 1975

Country of Service: Zaire (Congo)

Mission: United Methodist Board

Ministry: Pilot

Martyrdom: 1984, age 35, Moba, Lake Tanganyika

Stanley Gordon Ridgway

"Jesus will make it all right"

An Unwelcome Demand

"We want you to fly us to Moba on Lake Tanganyika," demanded one of two Zairian colonels as they stood at Stan's door. "We need to check on troops up there that have not been heard from for two days. There are rumors of rebels in that area, and we need to get there immediately to investigate. You are taking us there."

It was just about noon on a Tuesday. Stan had spent the morning catching up on flight-related paperwork. His plane "Charlie-Charlie" was out at the Lubumbashi airport readied for the next day's mission flying. The last thing he wanted to do was to fire it up to get involved in a potentially dangerous army rebel conflict. That's not why he had come to Zaire. He had come to serve the church and to this point had made every effort to steer clear of political entanglements.

Now he and his plane were being commandeered by high-ranking officers of the Zairian army. They were demanding that he fly into a volatile situation where he did not want to get involved.

"I don't have the fuel to make that long of a flight," he protested as an excuse. "It's four hundred miles to Moba, and I only have enough fuel for local flying."

"No problem," replied one of the colonels. "We will get the fuel. You get your plane ready."

With that the colonels sped away in their jeep and in less than twenty minutes had a truck following them, carrying two barrels of aviation gas. They had probably used their rank to confiscate the fuel. Now he had no alternative but to fly the two of them to Moba, a border town with Tanzania. He had noticed that they were heavily armed.

As the men took the aviation gas to the plane for fueling, Stan hurried back into the house to tell his wife, Linda, what was being demanded of him. She had just returned from shopping on behalf of the missionaries stationed in the interior and had not heard the exchange.

Good-bye

"I really don't want to make this flight," he told her. "Remember the last time I returned from Moba I told you there was rumor of a rebel incursion from Tanzania, across the lake? Well, it seems there must be real substance to that rumor. The colonels are insistent, and there is no way I can get out of it."

Linda's eyes widened as she heard him tell what he was being forced to do. She quickly went about fixing a sack lunch for him, knowing in her heart this unusual flight demand was fraught with danger. She had just enough time to finish, give him a big hug, and hear a tender "I love you" before he was out the door. Her eyes followed him as he made his way out the drive and headed to the airstrip. She had watched him leave many times before, but this time felt different.

While Stan was driving the short distance to the airport, his ground crew was hand-pumping the aviation gas from the drums into the wing tanks of the Cessna 210. They arranged the seat configuration for the two officers and finally untied the ropes that anchored the plane to the tarmac. As Stan pulled up to the plane he saw that it was nearly ready to go. Even though the soldiers were anxious to get going, he took time to do the preflight inspection as any well-taught pilot would. This was automatic for him, having been trained at the Moody aviation program in Elizabethton, Tennessee.

First he walked around the plane, visually inspecting and periodically touching its body and then the prop. Next, he climbed a short ladder, opened the fuel cap at the top of the wing, and using a dipstick, measured to see that the tanks were indeed full. He climbed down, went under the wing, and pushed a narrow glass beaker up against a small nozzle, squirting a sample of fuel into the glass. Satisfied there were no water or impurities in the fuel, he turned to the waiting officers and told them they could get on board. He motioned to them to put their gun belts and automatic rifles in the compartment behind them.

The Flight

Once his passengers were strapped in their seats, Stan tugged on their seat belts, checking to see that they were properly secured. Satisfied, he swung into the pilot seat, strapped on his helmet, and called to Linda through its attached microphone. Ever since he began flying in Zaire eight years earlier, Linda had been his flight follower, tracking his every move. He knew she would especially be there this time listening for his preflight call—and she was. Satisfied that the connection was good, he stuck his head out his side window and shouted "Clear!" One of the ground crew, standing to the front left of the plane and holding a fire extinguisher, signaled a thumbs-up "okay," and Stan started the engine. At first there were the typical three or four chugging burps, and then the engine fired into full life, causing the plane to rear up as if raring to go. It was 12:30 p.m.

Stan taxied the plane down to the far end of the runway. He turned it into the slight breeze, positioning the plane dead center on the end facing due east. Pulling his window shut, he spoke into his mike, identifying himself to the Lubumbashi airport control tower. He summarized his flight plan and was immediately granted clearance. He finished going through his checklist, eyed the control panel's gauges and dials one last time, twisted the steering column to the right and left, pushed it in and out, then simultaneously taking his feet off the brake pedals, with his right hand pushed the throttle in all the way. The Cessna went hurling down the runway and into the air well before reaching the strip's midpoint. The wheels quickly retracted into its belly.

Once airborne the plane smoothly sailed up into the sky. Stan banked the climbing plane to the left for about ten seconds and then set out on a NNE heading toward his destination. At the same time he radioed Linda that he was off the ground. After climbing for several minutes to reach the desired altitude, Stan pulled back on the throttle and adjusted the trim and ailerons so the plane could cruise level. He calculated that the four-hundred-mile flight to Moba would take two and a half hours.

With the busyness of getting airborne behind him, he now had a moment for reflection. He thought back to his childhood days as a missionary kid growing up in Bolivia. He had ridden in mission airplanes before he could ever remember. As a youngster his heroes were missionary pilots. His toys were airplanes. Every time he got into a plane he determined that he too would be a missionary pilot when he grew up. Now here he was a veteran missionary pilot of eight years.

"Please Be Careful"

Stan snapped back to the present. With his left thumb he pushed the button on the steering yoke to talk again to Linda.

"Ground base, this is Charlie-Charlie. I'm on a heading of zero-two-zero; altitude 7000 feet; winds are calm and sky is clear; ETA Moba fifteen hundred hours."

"Roger, copy, Charlie-Charlie," came Linda's quick reply. "Do you think you will be able to make a speedy turnaround and make it back home this evening?" she asked.

"Hard to say. I would like to discharge my passengers without shutting down the engine and immediately get out of there. But they may demand I stay for their inspection, and if they do, I will have to overnight."

"Roger, copy," she replied. She couldn't hide her disappointment.

The couple first met when both were students at Trinity Junior College (now Trinity Western University). Since Stan's parents were Canadian, it was the logical school for him to do his pre-aviation studies before going on to the Moody aviation program. Linda was from California, and not only was she physically appealing to him, but he saw a match in her spiritual demeanor as well. She too was interested in Christian missions. When he left to go to Moody for his aviation training, she returned to California to work at MAF (Mission Aviation Fellowship) headquarters. Now they were ten years married, had three children, ages seven, five, and two, and he loved her more than ever.

An hour into the flight Stan gazed off to the west. The village of Kasaji was somewhere in the far distance. That place would bring back memories too—horrid memories of when he almost lost his life and when one of his passengers did. There, five years ago, he had the most harrowing experience in his flying career. He remembered all too well the day he was flying in a different plane with five passengers and was attempting a mail drop over the mission station. It was raining and windy at the time, and visibility was poor. As he swooped in to make the drop, the plane hit a wind sheer throwing it earthward and almost hitting the ground. He was barely able to recover, but as he did and went to clear a wall of trees, the landing gear caught in the treetops, flinging the plane to the ground in a mangled crash. Upon impact it burst into flames as fuel gushed from its ruptured tanks.

Freeing himself from the burning wreckage, he had made a frantic effort to rescue his passengers. Even with the pain of three compressed vertebra, he quickly worked through the flames and was able to get four of the five passengers out before it was too late. In the process he suffered burns over 30 percent of his body. His face and hands were especially severely burnt.

In critical condition aboard the rescue helicopter, he told the pilot to send a fretting Linda the message, "Jesus will make it all right." The road to recovery was long. Stan, on a stretcher, and his family returned to North America and stayed for over two years so that he could receive proper medical care.

"Charlie-Charlie to base," Stan radioed.

"Base to Charlie-Charlie. What is your position?" Linda inquired.

"I am about twenty minutes out and should be landing at the previously given ETA. I have been thinking about the situation, and I want you to contact the American Consul General and make them aware of what is happening. They need to know I have been forced into making this flight against my will."

"Roger, copy, will do," responded an increasingly nervous Linda.

As the plane approached Moba, Stan decided to take the precaution of circling the village to look for signs of trouble. He told Linda that there were people in the Catholic mission compound and that things looked normal there. He then circled the small harbor that fronted the edge of the lake and reported that things looked normal there as well.

"I am going on in to land. I'm now setting up for my final approach."

"Copy, Charlie-Charlie, please be careful," came Linda's reply.

Stan adjusted the plane's flaps and pushed the rudder pedal to the right to align the plane squarely with the strip and then dropped the landing gear. Once down over it, he pulled back on the steering column and simultaneously cut back on the throttle. A normal high-pitched buzzing sound went off that warned of an impending stall just before the tires rumbled on the grass. After rolling about fifty yards, he pushed on the break pedals, bringing the plane to a full stop. The plane dipped slightly forward, then stood firm.

Into the Trap

Stan quickly scanned every direction, trying to spot any sign of rebels. He knew that if he saw any, he had enough strip left for a quick takeoff. He detected none. He began taxiing the plane over to a crude building that functioned as a terminal.

"Charlie-Charlie on the ground and taxiing toward the terminal. No sign of rebels, but we can't be certain they are not here. There are many places for them to conceal themselves around the strip."

"Copied that," replied Linda. "What is your plan?"

"I intend to keep the engine running while disembarking the passengers and then quickly get airborne."

"Yes, please make it quick."

After reaching the front of the terminal, Stan brought the plane to a halt and, while still seated, flung open the passenger door behind him using the inside handle. He intended to stay tight in the cockpit and let the passengers leave the plane on their own. But then he noticed movement coming toward the plane—dozens of camouflaged figures pointing weapons. Stan realized they had been surrounded after all. He had flown right into their trap.

"Linda, the plane has been surrounded . . . " were the final words she heard.

No Word

Linda spent a fretful evening and sleepless night wondering what had happened to her husband. She, along with others in the mission community, stayed glued to the radio all night awaiting word from Stan or of Stan's fate. Nothing ever came. By 11:00 the following morning, she and the other Methodist missionaries knew for certain something was indeed wrong. Stan had not been heard from. The army officers had not been heard from. The local Christians on the ground had not been heard from. Nothing but static hummed through the radio.

The prolonged silence confirmed to the Zairian army that rebels had indeed overrun the area. They immediately mobilized and launched an air assault, dropping three hundred paratroopers into the area. Once on the ground the troops successfully beat back the insurgents, killing over one hundred in the fighting that ensued. Only when a detachment finally reached the airstrip did the fate of Stan become known. Witnesses later supplied the details.

One Last Flight

When the gun-pointing rebels surrounded the plane, the two colonels were forced out and immediately taken prisoner. Stan was ordered to get out as well, which he did, but he left the plane's engine running. After taking them a short distance away, the rebels pushed the two colonels to the ground and started tying them up. Seeing this, Stan turned and began making his way back to the plane, probably to turn off the engine. As he turned to climb into the plane, the rebels opened fire. His body dropped next to the plane. His spirit took one last flight. Several days later the airstrip was recaptured, and Stan's bullet-ridden body was recovered along with those of the two colonels.

Stan was no stranger to Moba. He had flown many flights into that lakeside town. He knew the local Methodist believers wanted to erect a church building, so he had helped with its planning and supplies. It was this group of believers who reverently buried Stan's body four days after his death. It was these same believers who two years later proudly dedicated a new thousand-seat church building and medical clinic in his name as a memorial to him.

SOUTHEAST ASIA

Born: July 11, 1901, Eau Claire, Wisconsin

Nationality: American

Graduated from Moody: 1925

Country of Service: Philippines

Mission: American Baptist Foreign Mission Society

Ministry: Pioneer evangelist

Martyrdom: 1943, age 42, Panay Island

Erle Frederick Rounds

"We can meet again in that land which is fairer than day"

"These mountain trips seem to satisfy an inner urge to get away from the soft life of our modern civilization and take our chances on the trail with the simple, unsophisticated mountain people, sleeping in their houses, eating their food, and meeting them on their own ground,"[1] wrote Erle Rounds. The mountains and the mountain people on the island of Panay, Philippines, were pioneer evangelist Erle Rounds's parish. He loved every bit of this rugged ministry to unreached tribal peoples in the interior of the island.

Built like an athlete and gifted with a pioneering spirit, Erle could endure long forays over mountain trails and staying overnight in tiny, primitive huts. His singular goal was to make Christ known in parts where His love had yet to be proclaimed. Reporting on these travels, Erle stated that the mountain people "were impressed that we were willing to walk for miles through rice paddies, on muddy paths, climbing over steep, slippery trails through rain and heat, and sometimes even crawling through tunnels caused by the wind blowing the tall tigbaw grass over the trails, and taking our chances by crossing flooding rivers—all to tell them about Christ."[2] But pioneer ministry had not always been Erle's passion in life.

Childhood

Born in Eau Claire, Wisconsin, in 1901, Erle was brought up in a Christian home and a Baptist church. At the age of twelve he was led to personal faith in Christ by his pastor. However, as a high school student, his athleticism on both the football field and the basketball court, as well as his good looks, brought him popularity that negatively influenced him. He slipped away from his Christian heritage and after high school spent months working on a surveying crew in Montana. This separation took him farther from his home, his church, and his Christian roots. He then entered Wisconsin State Normal School and for two years continued in his selfish, sinful ways.

Turn Around

Then beautiful, blonde-haired Louise Cummings entered his life and turned it around. A devout Christian, Louise challenged Erle to change his ways or else she would break off the relationship. This was a hard choice for Erle, and he fought it for a long time. Finally, in desperation he surrendered himself to God. He decided to go to Chicago to attend Moody Bible Institute for Bible training. This was a major turning point in his life. Erle would say of this decision:

> I made up my mind that I was going to get back the satisfaction that I had known before or bust in the attempt. I felt greatly indebted to the Bible Institute for the fine friendships and the way in which their instructors opened the Bible to me. It was through contact with one of the students there that I determined to get further training if it was only to finish up my Normal School work.[3]

Erle was at Moody from 1923–25, and then spent a year finishing up his studies at Wisconsin State Normal. He married Louise, and the two of them went to Berkeley, California, where they supervised Chinese boys at the Chung Mei home for Chinese boys for a year. Their first son was born the following year, and they decided that Erle should study at Berkeley Baptist Divinity School. He graduated in 1930 with the Th.B. and a strong leading by God to become a missionary.

"In the Master's Harvest Field"

During his final year at Berkeley, Erle and Louise applied to the American Baptist Foreign Mission Society. Wanting to make clear his call to foreign service to the board, Erle wrote:

> My only motive for seeking foreign missionary service is that I might find a place in the Master's harvest field. My friends and counselors have often said that I should seek foreign service. I see the need and have the personal conviction of the whole aim and purpose of foreign missions. I feel that I have the ability to meet the need. That is the reason I have felt led to make this step towards application and appointment to foreign service.[4]

Events moved quickly for the Roundses at that point. They were accepted by the board in May 1930, Erle was ordained that same month, they were commissioned by their church in August, and then the family of three sailed directly to the Philippines.

Erle proved himself to be a spirited missionary. Upon completion of language study, he and Louise thrust themselves into the work. For the first five years they ministered out of the city of San Jose on the island of Panay. Gifted as a pastor and a motivator of others, Erle took up a variety of roles. The Baptist leadership appointed him as the general provincial pastor and advisor to the Philippine pastors and workers for the area. He also worked with the youth in San Jose and did evangelistic touring as well as holding field conferences.

Following furlough in 1936, the Roundses, now with two young sons, centered their ministry at the American Baptist hospital at Capiz on the island of Panay. From this base, Erle made frequent evangelistic trips into the interior of the island, trekking into the isolated tribes that dotted the rugged mountainous terrain. While he made visits to remote villages, Louise managed a dormitory for high school girls and visited homes in the surrounding territory. Their mission experience could not have been better until the unexpected happened. On December 7, 1941, Pearl Harbor was bombed.

World War II

Less than a month after the bombing of Pearl Harbor, the Japanese invaded the Philippines. Manila fell on January 2. The Roundses' teenage son Donal, in Manila for schooling, was taken captive and interned along with many other Americans. With no avenue for escape, the Baptist missionaries associated with the Capiz hospital, including the Roundses, kept the hospital open until April when the Japanese finally reached their island. To avoid capture, the eleven missionaries took flight into the mountains to a site they had previously selected and prepared for this eventuality. A few other expatriate Americans connected with a nearby mining company joined them, making the population of the camp in the twenties at times.

The missionaries gave the name "Hopevale" (valley of hope) to their hideout, where they had carved a small clearing near the top of a remote mountain in the deep recesses of evergreens. Hopevale could only be reached by a winding and often misleading trail, and thus it was next to impossible for the Japanese to discover. Here they hid out for over a year and a half. The local population secretly kept them supplied with necessities, and that generosity is what sustained them. Erle, being a leader, became chaplain of the group.

At the same time they were hiding, Colonel Peralta sent word around the islands that all able-bodied free Americans were to join the guerrilla resistance against the Japanese. These men were not to be enlisted as combatants, but rather to help with the technical and intelligence side of the struggle. Erle joined up and was appointed to the rank of lieutenant and as a chaplain to the guerrilla force operating throughout the Panay interior. This new role kept him absent from Hopevale for extended periods of time as he was called upon to provide spiritual services for the guerrilla force. His God-given athleticism made him fit and able for the task. For over a year he trekked the mountain trails unarmed and much of the time barefoot and with minimal food, fulfilling his roles to the resistance, to the Christian villagers, and to the refugees at Hopevale.

The Hopevale Massacre

After an extended absence, early on Sunday morning December 19, 1943, Erle strolled into Hopevale to join his family for Christmas. However, no sooner had he reunited with Louise and nine-year-old Erle Junior than the camp was attacked by a force of five hundred Japanese soldiers. Caught by surprise, everyone in the camp attempted to flee. Vainly each tried to scramble into the nearby brush where they had emergency hideouts, but within an hour the Japanese were able to round up all the missionaries. A few from the mining company did escape, causing the Japanese to wait a day before doing anything with their captives. Those who escaped were never found, and this infuriated the Japanese.

The missionaries speculated that they would be taken to a concentration camp, as had happened to some of their coworkers previously captured from another hospital. What a shock it was when Captain Kunoyi Watanabe informed them that he was under orders to execute them all! One of the missionaries who spoke fluent Japanese pleaded for their lives, but to no avail. Instead, Watanabe gave them an hour to prepare before beginning the executions.

Starting with the oldest, the beheadings began. To dramatize the event, one by one the eleven prisoners were blindfolded and then systematically led to the designated hut. Once inside they were commanded to bow and then swiftly were decapitated by the same Samurai sword. Erle, Louise, and their coworkers were thus summarily executed.

When finished with the killings, the Japanese burned the hut to hide the evidence. According to a Filipino eyewitness, Erle Junior and two other children were killed by bayonet separately in a nearby hut. Erle and Louise were mercifully spared the sight and knowledge of their young son's death. After the Japanese had left, Filipino Christians recovered the remains of the slain and buried them beneath the altar at Hopevale's outdoor chapel.

"Worthy of the World . . . and That Other Land"

In one of Erle's last letters before fleeing to the mountains he had written to the mission headquarters:

> We are living in interesting times over here, and I believe the missionaries are going to see real persecution before the thing is over. . . . But it is one of the greatest privileges I can think of to be here as a missionary. . . . We hope to see you all again, but, if we should be denied that blessed joy, we can meet again in that land which is fairer than day. May we strive harder to be worthy of the world which God has given us and of that other land made possible through our Lord Jesus Christ.[5]

Erle and Louise Rounds, along with the others, were found to be worthy of that land which is fairer than day.

1 *Through Shining Archway,* 39.

2. Ibid., 40.

3. Erle Rounds, personal letter, 1.

4. Ibid., 2.

5. *Through Shining Archway,* 42.

Born: April 20, 1898, Akeley, Pennsylvania

Nationality: American

Attended Moody: 1923–1924

Country of Service: Philippines

Mission: American Baptist Foreign Mission Society

Ministry: Teacher of religious education

Martyrdom: 1943, age 45, Panay Island

Signe Amelia Erickson

"I have been charmed with the people"

"My first desire to be a foreign missionary came while I was a child in Sunday school. It had been my mother's desire too, and when she couldn't go, she prayed that one of her children might become a missionary. My main motive for foreign service is that I might carry the gospel of Christ to those who are hungry and waiting for it. Unless I believe that God could use me as an instrument in bringing them to Christ I would not want to go. When I compare the number of Christian workers in India, Assam, or Burma, to the number per person in our own country, I should feel very selfish in not going to those whose need is so much greater than ours."[1] So wrote Signe to the directors of the American Baptist Foreign Mission Society as she sought their approval for service. Subsequently, she was accepted and sailed to the Philippines in 1930.

After several months on the island of Panay, having had time to adjust to her new environment, she wrote back to the board, "From the very first I have been charmed with these beautiful islands and with the people whom I have met. My love for the people and for the work grows as I learn to appreciate them more."[2] Signe began her missionary career as a teacher, something she would do until the end, and a profession for which she had been highly trained.

Early Years

Signe was born and raised in a pious Swedish home in the small village of Akeley nestled in the hills of northwestern Pennsylvania. Her parents helped lead her to Christ at age twelve. But as a teen she began to doubt her experience and fell away when she boarded with a non-Christian family during her high school years. She received her teacher's degree at Clarion State Normal School in 1918. Two years later she came back to the Lord during a series of revival meetings in the town where she was teaching.

Additional Training and Experience

This time Signe's commitment to the Lord was genuine. She was baptized and then joined Calvary Baptist Church of Warren, Pennsylvania. Sensing God leading her to missionary service, she entered Moody Bible Institute for a year's training in 1923. Academically astute and with perfectionist tendencies, she consistently scored high grades. During her time at Moody, she was noted as "a woman of sterling character, strong in spirit . . . strong personality, capable and earnest. Always abounding in good cheer."[3]

Following Moody, Signe proved her ability as a teacher by returning to the hills of western Pennsylvania and volunteering to take on a country school so notorious for its undisciplined students that three teachers in succession had resigned the previous year. Single-handedly she so mastered the unruly boys throughout the winter months that by spring their hearts were softened by her caring Christian example. Before she left, several came to faith in Christ.

Sensing the need for more training, Signe next went to Gordon College to earn a Bachelor of Theology degree and then added a year at Bethel Seminary. Confident that she was now prepared to teach overseas, she applied to and was accepted by the Women's American Baptist Foreign Missionary Society for work in the Philippines. She demonstrated her maturity and focus on missions by telling the board,

> The only message I have is the gospel message in all its fullness
> —1 Corinthians 15—the message of hope of immortality, the

message of abundant life with all the attendant blessings of peace, power and capacities for service which are given to those who surrender to Christ and His will for them. The medium of giving the gospel message would not be limited to preaching or teaching, but would include Christ-like living in their midst.[4]

Thirteen Fruitful Years

Signe arrived at the Baptist work on Panay Island in September 1930. She spent her first year at the Baptist Home School at Capiz. The following year she went to Iliolo to work with Dorothy Dowell who, as it turned out, would be her coworker the rest of her life. The two taught together at the Baptist Missionary Training School, preparing young women for church ministries and missionary work.

Always engaged in lifelong learning, during two successive furloughs Signe worked on a master's degree at Columbia University, New York. She returned to the field in May 1941 with her new degree in hand and a new vision for the work. As professor of religion at Central Philippine College in the School of Theology, she dedicated herself to the training of students for Christian ministry.

As war became more likely, Signe and Dorothy were under no illusion as to what the prospect of war could mean to them and their work. They frequently discussed what measures they would take if the Japanese were to invade the islands. Signe expressed the conviction that she wanted to stay with the Filipinos unless her continued presence endangered the lives of the people she had come to serve.

When the Japanese acted, they moved swiftly. First it was Pearl Harbor in December 1941. Then Japanese forces overran Manila in January 1942. By April they reached Panay Island and quickly overtook the cities of Capiz and Iliolo. Soon the entire coastal area of the island was in their grasp. Signe had no place of escape except to the interior of the island. She joined the other American Baptist missionaries in the mountain hideout they named Hopevale. Here she and the others waited out the war.

After a year in hiding, she was able to get a letter out that eventually reached America. In it she mentioned who was with her and the location of others who were also in hiding. She commented on the condition of her situation, saying:

> We have occasionally played hide-and-seek with the Japanese but have lived in this place from the beginning of our mountain life. We have excellent drinking water, live near a stream, are comfortable in our bamboo houses, do our own work, and when it is safe make occasional visits to nearby barrios for work that we may do there. . . . Our hearts have been deeply stirred by the generosity and devotion of friends and churches that have brought gifts of rice, chickens, bananas, coffee, and even money to us. . . . Please inform our friends, relatives, and families of our welfare. We are conscious of their concern for us and are grateful for their prayers for us.[5]

That was the last communication anyone would receive from Signe. As her seclusion passed from months to a year and then to a year and a half, the rigors of isolated living took their toll on her. She was now middle-aged, her clothes worn thread thin, and her shoes worn out altogether, leaving her barefooted. Her natural wavy hair turned gray, and she became thin and delicate in stature.[6] In her mountain hideaway Signe patiently hoped for either the end of the war or for rescue by American forces. As it turned out, neither happened in time to save either her or the others hiding from the Japanese.

Count Most for His Cause

The end of all hope came to Hopevale on a fateful December morning just days before Christmas in 1943. A battalion of Japanese soldiers crept through the mountains and made a surprise assault on the little hamlet. It took the soldiers less than an hour to round up all eleven unsuspecting missionaries who had been caught completely off guard. The Japanese waited a day to make sure they had caught everyone. They then told their captives that they were to be executed. The Japanese granted them an hour to prepare to die. Then systematically, one by one they were blindfolded and taken into a hut where they were ruthlessly beheaded. Signe's life ended in the midst of that heartless slaughter.

Two years previously, upon her return to the Philippines from her Stateside furlough, Signe had written a friend about what she anticipated during her next term of ministry. "I look forward to a term of fruitful service here, and pray God to use me in ways that will count most for His cause."[7] For reasons known only to Him, a year and a half in hiding and then a swift, cruel death was the way God used Signe most for His cause.

1. "Miss Signe A. Erickson," appointment letter, 2.
2. Personal letter, Signe Erickson, 1930.
3. Moody Bible Institute Academic Records, Signe Erickson.
4. *Through Shining Archway,* 28.
5. Personal letter, Signe Erickson, May 15, 1943.
6. For a description of the conditions Signe and the others endured, an excellent account of those final days can be found in the book *Guerrilla Wife,* by Louise Spencer, one of the survivors.
7. *Through Shining Archway,* Ibid.

Born: July 17, 1927, Luzon, Philippines

Nationality: Filipino

Graduated from Moody: 1958

Country of Service: Vietnam

Mission: Wycliffe Bible Translators

Ministry: Bible translator

Martyrdom: 1963, age 35, Highway 20, near Dalat

Alfonso Gaspar Taqueban Makil

"Few have ever heard of Christ. I must go."

Gaspar Makil has the distinction of being the only Moody martyr to whom tribute was paid by a head of state. Following Gaspar's death in 1963, Ferdinand Marcos, then president of the Philippines, said of him,

> Not all stars shine with equal brilliance. Some wink remotely in the heavens, others swing low and bright in the sky. Men's lives do not all glow alike. Not all are like the men of history whose lives still influence people and nations. But in a world still enshrouded by dark nights of crime, greed, and selfishness, humanity is thankful for each individual, however humble, who helps to dispel darkness in some way, through a life dedicated to the service of others. Such men and women are heroes too. Alfonso Gaspar Taqueban Makil, a Filipino, was such a man.[1]

Vietnam and the Philippines, countries that face each other across the South China Sea, have many things in common. Both contain rugged mountainous terrain, beautiful lakes, and mighty rivers. Both have an abundance of palm trees that dot sandy beaches next to deep blue seas. Both have populations that are about equal in number, with millions living in large cities and millions of others scattered in rural villages. Historically, both had been colonized by European Catholic nations. Both enjoy lush tropical weather. Both are composed of numerous ethnic groups, speaking distinct dialects. Both have need of Bible translations to make God's Word available in those many heart languages. Both were the world of Gaspar Makil, a trained Bible translator, who took his skills and abilities from one to the other.

Survival and WWII

Gaspar was born on the northern part of Luzon in July 1927. His father was a forester; his mother was a schoolteacher. They were Methodists who brought their eight children up in a nominally Protestant home. When he was nine months old, Gaspar was baptized by the Methodist Episcopal minister in Salcedo.

Life was rather idyllic for Gaspar in his growing-up years. The Makils didn't have much, but they always had enough. Pets and friends and parents and grandparents made Gaspar's life complete. All of that was shattered when he was fourteen and the Japanese invaded his island and his tranquil way of life. Enemy soldiers burned his village and his home and killed a cousin who tried to resist them.

At first as a young teenager, Gaspar could do little to resist the invaders. On the advice of his parents he continued attending school, but secretly had the job of keeping the ROTC rifles clean and hidden. Many nights he went to bed hungry so there would be enough food for the army. At age fifteen he joined the Red Lions, a Philippine army resistance unit, where he would eventually become a staff sergeant as the war continued for three more years. There were never enough supplies to go around, and he spent much of the war barefooted and on the run from the enemy.

One memorable event that had an impact on Gaspar during his military service was his part in helping liberate the Los Baños Internment camp. In a daring raid by the resistance army, he, along with his Red Lions, helped free 2,500 prisoners. Rescuing American Methodist missionaries Joseph Moore and his family left an indelible impression on him. Six months later the war was over, and Gaspar was discharged from the army.

Seeking and Finding

Gaspar returned home and finished high school. He spent the next ten years in various schools seeking to discover what life had for him. Eventually, his search would lead him to America and to God. After graduating from National University in Manila with a degree in mechanical engineering, through great sacrifice on the part of his family, he entered Southern Methodist University in 1954 in Dallas, Texas. Gaspar told his friends and family he was going to SMU to earn an advanced degree in engineering. But that was merely a cover-up for his real intent. Secretly, in his heart, he was on a search for something he thought would bring meaning to his empty life. He didn't really know what he was searching for or where his search would lead him. As a sincere seeker, he only knew that there must be more meaning to life.

Once on campus, Gaspar's search would not be long, because God's sovereignty directed him to Himself. Through the influence of companions who feared God and the campus InterVarsity chapter, Gaspar personally came to experience a new birth in Christ. He attended the Urbana missionary conference and left feeling compelled by God to give himself for missionary service. Gaspar's personal search was finally over. To his dying day his commitment to unreservedly follow Christ never wavered. To a friend he commented, "During the year 1954 and until the first part of 1955, the Lord narrowed down my interest from the thing that I came to the United States to do, giving me a desire, more and more, to learn more of Him, to study His word. That is how I finally wound up at the Moody Bible Institute in Chicago."[2]

Chicago and Marriage

Wanting to be well trained for Christian service, Gaspar left SMU and entered Moody in the fall of 1955. At first he intended to enroll in the missionary aviation program. But he was disappointed to learn that he could not pursue aviation training because the United States government forbade foreigners from acquiring a US pilot license. Undeterred, he switched to the pastoral course. Over the next three years he devoted himself to studying as much Bible, theology, and as many biblical languages as the program allowed.

Life was not easy for Gaspar while at Moody. He struggled with finances and many times skimped on meals to make ends meet. He worked for meager pay as a night janitor in a beauty salon the entire three years. The generosity of his friends back at SMU kept him going. Eventually, he graduated in June of 1958.[3]

Following graduation, Gaspar did not have a clear idea of what he should do, but was open and ready to wherever the Lord would lead him. He spent the year as a Chicago Transit Authority bus driver while he waited. As he did, the Lord brought a bright young girl into his life who would change him forever. Josephine Johnson, an amazing African-American from Colorado, was working by day as a switchboard operator at the headquarters of InterVarsity Christian Fellowship, attending Moody classes at night, and playing the piano at a Filipino church held at the Pacific Garden Mission on Sundays. That was where Gaspar discovered her. Courtship blossomed into romance, which led to marriage in June of 1959.

Preparation and New Beginnings

As newlyweds, the Makils went to the Summer Institute of Linguistics school in North Dakota that summer. Gaspar soon discovered that he had a gift and a growing passion to do Bible translation. At summer's end before leaving North Dakota, he and Josephine applied to become members of Wycliffe Bible Translators. He made clear his belief in the priority of translation work on his application when he wrote:

The statement of Paul in Romans 15:20 (preach the gospel where Christ was not named) is a statement which I wish to adopt for doing pioneer work. . . . Perhaps it is a foregone conclusion to state that in order to be effective we must bring the gospel message in the language which the people can understand, the language through which they express their joys and pleasures, as well as their pain and sorrow, the lan guage through which they can be taught.[4]

The Makils were accepted by Wycliffe, sent to jungle training camp in Mexico, and had their first child, a son, all during the next twelve months. A daughter was born to them the following year. After a visit to his family in the Philippines, they arrived for their assignment in Vietnam in March of 1962. The determination and perhaps premonition of hardship by Gaspar was expressed in a letter to his pastor in Chicago just before leaving:

I am ready to go. I believe it is God's will for my life, but I am afraid, somehow not for myself, but for my dear wife and for my children. But men are dying over there without Christ; few have ever heard of Him. I must go. Pray for me.[5]

Little could Gaspar and Josephine know the tragedy that would strike them before reaching their first anniversary on the field. Energetically, they set out doing all the things new missionaries do: studied the Vietnamese language and culture; set up house in the town of Dran close to Dalat; and got acclimated to the people, geography, and climate. Just a few months after arrival, they had the added joy of welcoming twin girls, Janie and Jessie, into their world.

At the end of January 1963, the Makils went to Saigon to arrange birth certificates for the twins, get medical checkups, and prepare for a tribal language survey in south-central Vietnam. The purpose of the tribal language survey was to determine for what language they were to do a translation. In time Southern Roglai, a Malayo-Polynesian language spoken by forty thousand people, was chosen as their focus.

Vietcong and Death

On March 4 at 7:30 in the morning, the entire Makil family, along with coworkers Elwood and Vurnell Jacobsen, set out in a Land Rover on the six-hour trip back to Dran. At about 10:00 a.m., after traveling sixty-six miles north of Saigon, they came to a roadblock. Other vehicles were stopped ahead of them. Armed men motioned them to stop too. Assuming it was a government checkpoint, they stopped and showed their identification cards. They were then commanded to leave their vehicle and stand by the side of the road with the others. Only then did the missionaries realize that the men who stopped them were black-trousered Vietcong.

As they stood waiting to see what would happen next, a warning shot was heard in the forest. A government army truck suddenly came into view farther up the road. The Vietcong, taken by surprise, indiscriminately began firing their weapons on the bystanders they had pulled from the cars. Elwood was killed immediately, taking a shot to the head.

Gaspar had his son, Thomas, and baby Janie in his arms at the moment the firing began. Taken by surprise, he too was cut down by automatic fire, hit several times in the chest and also in the jugular vein. He fell to the ground, dying instantly. Thomas and Janie were also hit. Thomas survived a leg wound, but five-month-old Janie died later that night. The Vietcong were routed and the area secured by government forces.

Two days later memorial services were held at the Tan Son Nhut airbase, Saigon, for the three who were slain. Mourners from the entire mission community joined in paying last respects to fellow workers. Since both Gaspar and Elwood were veterans, their caskets were draped with their respective national flags. Elwood was buried outside of Saigon. Gaspar's and Janie's bodies were flown to the Philippines.

Response and Commitment

Gaspar and Elwood were the first missionaries to be killed in the Vietnam War, which at that point was still in its infant stage. When the Vietcong realized they had unknowingly killed unarmed missionaries, they issued a quick apology. "We thought they were government workers. We didn't know they were missionaries," agents told people in surrounding villages.[6]

Upon hearing the news of their deaths, many letters poured into Wycliffe expressing both sorrow and deeper commitment to follow Christ. Some eventually did follow through on those commitments and joined the work of Wycliffe.

Josephine continued serving with distinction in the mission until her death in 2003. Initially she transferred to the Wycliffe Philippine headquarters, where she could both work and be close to her in-laws. Later she became a recruiter in the States, where she was especially influential in recruiting African-Americans into Bible translation work.[7]

1. Felicia S. Brichoux, *Gaspar the Second King*, foreword.
2. Ibid., 47.
3. Moody Bible Institute Academic Records, Gaspar Makil.
4. Brichoux, 71–72.
5. Ibid., 97.
6. James and Marti Hefley, *By Their Blood*, 120.
7. http://www.wycliffe.org/africanamerican/makilj.htm

LATIN AMERICA

Born: January 8, 1896, Worcester, Massachusetts

Nationality: American

Graduated from Moody: 1922

Country of Service: Brazil

Mission: Inland South American Union

Ministry: Pioneer church planter

Martyrdom: 1930, age 34, Juruena

Arthur Francis Tylee

"I am in the will of God"

Arthur sat at his desk in his comfortable study at Harvard Law School, unable to shake the undeniable call of God in his life. His inner soul was restless, because the longer he studied at Harvard, the more he felt out of place. The son of wealthy New England parents, he was here in the setting both he and his parents had planned all along—studying at the most prestigious law school in the country. His father had planned for him to become a corporate lawyer. Yet Arthur felt unfulfilled. He knew God had something greater for him than to litigate on behalf of multimillion-dollar companies for the rest of his life.

The demanding academic load was not a problem. Arthur was a proven scholar. He had excelled in studies both at Amherst College and at Besançon University in France. He had an unusual gift for languages and by now was fluent in five. He had been given the highest educational advantages and had proven himself worthy. Yet, deep inside Arthur felt unfulfilled. So he decided to set aside special time for reading his Bible and for prayer. While reflecting on the Scriptures, his soul grieved as he pondered the plight of the lost "without God and without hope" who were dying by the thousands daily in their darkness. His conviction grew that if he was meant for something greater than the pursuit of temporal riches, his purpose was to be found in the service of his Lord. Arthur packed his belongings, left Harvard, and announced to his family that he intended to become a missionary. He entered Moody Bible Institute to train for that purpose.

To War and Back

Arthur was born in Worcester, Massachusetts, on January 8, 1896. Raised in a Baptist home, he accepted Christ as his Savior at the age of fifteen. During his college years he strayed from his faith, accepting liberal classroom teachings that rejected the Bible as having any authority over the affairs of mankind. But then World War I forced him to reconsider. As a young enlisted man, he was sent to the front in France in 1918. Because of his training, he was reassigned to work at General Headquarters, assisting the allied commanders who were directing the war. After the signing of the armistice, he was given the privilege of attending the University of Besançon while still in France. Upon his return to the States, he entered Harvard Law School before turning his back on that prestigious education and moving on to Moody in 1920.

Studies at Moody

Throughout his two years at Moody, Arthur was a standout not only in his studies but also in the esteem and respect he earned from fellow students. "Ty," as they affectionately nicknamed him, became a leader in Institute activities, was particularly active at the South American Prayer Band, and was chairman of the Student Volunteers. The summary on his academic record sheds light on his reputation: "Excellent in every way—educational, character, spiritual life, missionary fervor. One of our best and most promising graduates."[1]

While at Moody, Arthur became acquainted with another student, Ethel Canary from Memphis, Tennessee. Besides her charm, a compelling virtue that drew Ethel to his attention was her dedication to missions. She already had two sisters serving in China, and she herself was deputation secretary in Chicago for the Mission to the

Lepers. The two became engaged and would be married three years later after both had arrived in South America.

Contacting the Nhambiquara

Arthur arrived in South America in June 1923 as a member of the Inland South America Missionary Union (now South America Mission or SAM). Beginning with a few weeks in Argentina and then a stint of service in Paraguay, he finally reached Brazil a few months later. Hearing of the wild, unreached Nhambiquara tribe deep in the heart of the Amazon jungle, Arthur made it his passion to win this tribe for Christ. After months of studying Portuguese, Arthur was ready to contact the tribe.

In May of 1924 he and another missionary formed an expeditionary party and set out to contact the Nhambiquara. They experienced seventy-four frustrating days as they tirelessly carved their way over land through the jungle and marsh. Only five days were without showers of rain. Their five oxen were most exasperating, causing them to lose whole days or to gain only a hundred yards or so per day.

Adding to the hardship were the multitudinous insects that pestered them every step of the way. After two months they finally reached the telegraph line two hundred miles inland and found it would be useless to continue on to Juruena, their goal, still another hundred miles beyond. However, before turning back they were able to meet up with a party of Nhambiquara. Stark naked and slender with bronze skin and straight black hair, they looked every bit the part of the wild men they were reported to be. The two men explained to the Nhambiquara why they had come and then told them they would return again in the future to live among them.

The pioneering spirit of Arthur is seen in a letter written to his fiancée, Ethel, after the trip.

My feelings at the first contact with these naked and savage people would be hard to describe. As a boy I used to bemoan the fact that I had not lived in the wild Indian days such as are depicted in the stories of early New England. Later when looking toward pioneer mission work here, I feared that I was too late to ever engage in work with those who were absolutely uncivilized. But here was a raw article; the Indian; the absolutely uncivilized Indian. Instead of repulsion or fear, such a feeling of love toward them rose within me that it seemed as though I must tell them how much I loved them. And how God loved them even to the giving of His Son for them. From that day to this, the longing to make this message known to them, to live with them, an example and a help to them by the grace of God, increases rather than diminishes.[2]

Sufficiently recovered from their first jungle foray, in January 1925 Arthur and William Hunrichs started out a second time to reach the Nhambiquara. They first launched out by boat and then went by foot again through the mucky jungle. It took three weeks to go the first thirty-two miles under disagreeable and trying conditions. By the last of April they reached their secondary objective, but because their supplies and strength were totally exhausted, they felt it best to return to their home base in Corumba. By June they made it back, and to Arthur's delight Ethel was there waiting for him. They were married three weeks later.

A week after their marriage Arthur and Ethel set out again to set up a mission station in Nhambiquara territory. After a grueling trek through the jungle that mirrored the previous two, they successfully arrived at Juruena, a lonely Brazilian telegraph outpost on the edge of Nhambiquara territory. They erected their station house and named it Maloquinha, "Little Village."[3] Hardship, privation, and near starvation were the Tylees' daily companions over the next year. Lack of proper nourishment caused by the shortage of food and climatic conditions constantly threatened Arthur's health and, even harder for him to bear, that of his wife. On two separate occasions Ethel was close to death from malaria and beriberi.

Added to this was the constant threat of an uprising by the native people. The Nhambiquara temperament was unpredictable, and they never were without their machetes. Twice Arthur felt the blade of steel at his throat. However, Arthur and Ethel befriended the Nhambiquaras, traded with them, and began to master their language. After nearly a year on their own, a reinforcement finally arrived in the person of Albert McDowell. McDowell, from Ireland, noting the weakened and emaciated state of the Tylees, assured them he could look after the work while they took a much-needed leave.

Rest in the States

The Tylees spent the next two years back in the States recuperating from the past term and preparing themselves for the next. Besides visiting friends and supporters, they had a greater joy with the birth of their daughter, Marian Neill. Many well-meaning people pleaded with them to not take their precious baby back to the wild Amazon jungle. But Arthur insisted that as servants of the God who called them to reach the Nhambiquara, that was exactly what they planned to do.

The Tylees were effective recruiters too. Seven new missionaries sailed back with them on the *SS Southern Cross* in May 1928. Not all would work with them, since some were recruited for various other work in the mission. But they were particularly glad to have Mildred Kratz, a nurse, on board who would join them at Juruena.

Return to Brazil

Upon reaching their station, the Tylees could tell that much had changed during their two-year absence. For one thing, transportation had so improved that it only took them three weeks instead of three months to reach Juruena. For another, the ever-cautious Nhambiquara were beginning to get accustomed to outsiders. Instead of the timid, wary disposition of the past, they now came to the station much more frequently and for prolonged periods of time. They seemed to enjoy staying at the house and showed affectionate attention to the little white baby girl.

The Tylees now had coworkers too. Albert McDowell had stayed on and was making valuable contributions to the work. Mildred Kratz was there to tend to the medical needs of both the missionaries and the natives. A young Brazilian girl, Dona Maria, joined them to help with domestic work. A team was now in place, poised to reach the Nhambiquara.

Monday Morning Massacre

In the later part of 1929 and early 1930 a flu virus was brought into the area by Brazilian visitors. The virus quickly spread among the unprotected Nhambiquara. One of their number, Manoel, an influential leader, was treated by nurse Mildred Kratz, but eventually succumbed to the disease. The grieving friends tied Manoel's lifeless body onto the back of a fellow Nhambiquara and transported him back to his village. For months after that they stayed away, much to the disappointment of the Tylees.

Then in late October two events brought encouragement to the Tylees. One was Ethel's announcement that she was pregnant! Now little Marian would have a playmate to grow up with there in the jungle. The other was the reappearance of the Nhambiquara led by their chief, Capitao Joao.

By Sunday, November 2, forty of the natives had made their way to Maloquinha. They camped around the Tylee house and promised to work for Arthur the following day on a road he was building that would permit motor vehicles to drive in from the outside world. However, the Nhambiquara seemed a bit more hostile than previously. When Arthur offered one of their leaders to overnight in his house, the native angrily turned on his heals and said, "No, it is dangerous to stay here. Manoel died here."[4] Arthur assured him that Manoel had died there, but that he did not get sick there but was very ill when he was brought in. This incident was the first intimation that the native people were upset and blamed the missionaries for the death of Manoel. Yet the missionaries weren't too alarmed.

The next day the Nhambiquara showed up much earlier than usual. They sat quietly on the ground in small groups talking to one another in low voices. Capitao Joao, along with a few others, went into the house and ate breakfast with the Tylees and Mildred Kratz. He sat down right next to Arthur and casually talked throughout the meal with the unsuspecting Arthur.

When finished with breakfast, Arthur got up and went outside to start the work crews for the morning. He had barely gotten out the door when Capitao Joao let out a loud, shrill-sounding signal. The Nhambiquara in the yard quickly descended upon the surprised missionaries. Arthur was dealt a swift, strong, debilitating blow to the head. Staggering forward, he fell head first onto the porch unconscious. Arrows swiftly penetrated his body as he lay motionless.

Meanwhile in the house, all was in chaos. Ethel, seeing Mildred get pinned to a wall in the tight grip of an Indian, jumped up from the table to rush to her aid. Then, thinking of her two-year-old child still asleep in her bed, she instinctively ran toward Marian's bedroom.

As she did she was struck on the back of the head by a heavy hoe handle. She fell, tried to get up, but was struck two more times until unconscious. Her body rolled under the bed, where she was left for dead. The native men left the house believing they had killed all.

When Ethel regained consciousness, a deadly hush pervaded the house. She was in a daze and all was a blur. With blood streaming down her nose, mouth, and head wounds, she stumbled over to the crib and found baby Marian dead, an arrow thrust through her chest. She staggered over to where the body of Mildred lay on the floor and numbly pulled an arrow from the nurse's body. She knelt for a moment holding her lifeless friend in her arms. Then, thinking of Arthur, she crawled across the floor and out onto the porch. She found Arthur where he had fallen with a tranquil look on his face.

In all, six had been slain, counting the Brazilian coworkers. Ethel, the only one to survive the attack, painfully staggered for a mile to the telegraph station and reported what had happened. The operator telegraphed Albert McDowell, who was seventy miles downriver getting supplies. Upon hearing the tragic news, Albert made a hasty trip back to Juruena. He arrived by 9:00 p.m. and immediately cleansed and bandaged Ethel's wounds, which were still unattended. He marveled that she could have survived.

The next morning, along with some kindly Brazilians from the telegraph station, Albert laid the martyred bodies to rest in a grove of trees by a little brook across from the house. Baby Marian was placed in her father's arms as the two were lowered together into the ground. Arthur—soldier, scholar, servant—had entered his final rest.

The Grave Speaks Louder Than Life

Albert took Ethel to the coast for medical attention. Seven years would pass before another missionary would go back to Juruena.

Once there, he found only a few charred posts and a pile of ash-covered rocks marking the site where the massacre took place. However, he did discover that several of the Brazilians at the post had been converted through the witness of the martyrs' deaths. Today, seventy-five years later, one of the strongest churches among all the Brazilian native tribes where SAM works is the Nhambiquara tribal church.

After recovering from her wounds, Ethel returned to the States and delivered her second daughter, Mildred Frances Tylee, named after her martyred friend and her beloved husband. She spent her remaining years as a popular speaker in churches, Bible schools, and conferences as a catalyst for missions. Hundreds of young people presented themselves to missionary work through her impassioned pleas. She never remarried and died in 1955 at the age of sixty-one in Michigan.

Just before returning to Brazil for the last time, one of Arthur's cousins remarked when she realized the barbarous nature of the people to whom he would minister, "Cousin Arthur, these Indians may kill you." To which he calmly replied, "Suppose they do?" "But," she said, "you are going to give up your life," to which he replied, "I have nothing to do with how long I shall live. I am in the will of God. If He sees fit to let me live to complete the language and to present the Lord Jesus and His power to save, I shall be happy. If not, His will be done. Do you not know, dear cousin, that a grave often speaks louder than life?"[5]

1. Moody Bible Institute Academic Records, Arthur Tylee.

2. Joseph A. Davis, "In Memoriam Arthur Francis Tylee, an Appreciation," 2.

3. Ibid.

4. James and Marti Hefley, *By Their Blood,* 586.

5. Arthur Tylee, unpublished letter, 2.

Born: April 17, 1899, Cedar Rapids, Iowa

Nationality: American

Graduated from Moody: 1923

Country of Service: Brazil

Mission: Inland South American Union

Ministry: Nurse

Martyrdom: 1930, age 31, Juruena

Mildred Pauline Kratz

"Faithful and dependable"

In the minds of the Nhambiquara people it was a matter of determining who had more power—their witch doctor or the missionaries. In the mind of the newly arrived American missionary, Mildred Kratz, a registered nurse, it was a matter of giving the stricken patient proper medical care. Mildred had arrived with the Tylees at the isolated outpost of Juruena in the heart of the Amazon at the end of July 1930. She had known Arthur and Ethel Tylee when the three of them were students together at Moody. All along she had wanted to work with them on the mission field. Now, eight years later, on her very first day at the station, she was confronted with an important patient needing her care.

Grave Illness

Manoel was a Nhambiquara of considerable influence. His health had become undermined by weeks of illness while the Tylees were away from the area bringing Mildred to the station. Now they were back, and he lay precariously ill. Mildred, knowing this would be a test of her training as a missionary nurse, gave special attention to Manoel, treating his flu and apparent pneumonia the best she could. To her relief, the next day Manoel improved, but the following day he relapsed back into a critical state. Mildred became alarmed. He was no longer responding to her care.

Impatient, the native people watching over Manoel became upset and began to blame the missionaries. First they said the sickness was caused by the food the missionaries fed them. Arthur replied that they had all eaten the same food, and no one else was sick. Next they turned their blame on Mildred and the medicine she was giving him.

The accusation was quite natural, since as a newcomer they had yet no reason to trust her. The missionaries answered that others being treated by Mildred's medicine were improving. Finally, with all their arguments silenced, they calmed down and said that if Manoel died they would assure the relatives back in his village that the missionaries were not to blame. As it turned out, this promise would be an empty one.

Manoel did not improve. In fact, throughout the day he got worse. His people decided it was time to take matters into their own hands. Early in the evening they took Manoel outside. To either encourage him or to frighten away the evil spirits—the missionaries didn't know which—some of his Nhambiquara friends sat around him and began to sing. Struggling, Manoel sat up, gasping for breath as the others encircled him in song by the light of the fire. He sat on an animal hide, covered with a blanket; the firelight glistening on the brown bodies encircled him. The sky above was ablaze with stars.

At about eleven o'clock Manoel let out one last shrill cry. Then with all eyes watching, he lay down in silence. His spirit had passed into eternity. For Mildred and the other missionaries, this was the first death they had witnessed of a Nhambiquara. It broke her heart as she helplessly sat and listened to the tribal people break out in mourning. In the grip of fear, the awful fear of death, they hopelessly cried for the one who had passed into the unknown.

Years of Preparation

Mildred had prepared well for her profession as a missionary nurse. Born in 1899 in Cedar Rapids, Iowa, she was raised in a Christian home. She attended the local Congregational church with her family. After high school she went to Coe College and then entered Moody Bible Institute in September 1921.

She intended to study for only one year at Moody. However, gaining an appreciation for the education she was getting, she stayed on until graduating in 1923. It was during this time that Mildred came to know and respect two fellow classmates who were heading to the mission field. Arthur Tylee, Ethel Canary, and Mildred had become good friends. The three of them made plans to serve together in tribal missions. Little could they realize the cost that commitment would take.

Mildred involved herself in a variety of ministries such as hospital visitation, open evangelism, a home for elderly women, and even Chinese evangelism. These experiences helped her to grow in strength of purpose to the point that it was noted on her academic records, "Good personality. Energetic, enthusiastic, will make a splendid missionary or young people's worker. Faithful and dependable."[1]

Following graduation Mildred entered medical training at Augustana Hospital in Chicago and after two years received her degree as a registered nurse. She returned to Cedar Rapids to be with her widowed mother and practice nursing. She kept abreast of the efforts of the Tylees in Brazil as they pioneered the work among the Nhambiquara. When the Tylees returned to the States on furlough, she was able to meet with them and was accepted by Inland South America Missionary Union (now South America Mission) so that she could join them on their return. She sailed to Brazil with the Tylees on the *SS Southern Cross* in May 1928.

By early 1929 Mildred was on her way for the first time to the mission station at Juruena. Along the way they stopped at Utiarity, where the native people joined them in a meeting one night. Mildred noticed that one of the men had a cold, so she proceeded to treat her first Nhambiquara patient. Teaching him how to gargle was a chore, but he soon learned it perfectly and became well. Through this experience Mildred became confident that she had an important role to play in helping this poor, unreached people group.

Spiritual Conflict

It was just a few days after Mildred arrived at Juruena that she would care for one of the most important patients in her brief five-month missionary career. Manoel, a much-beloved Nhambiquara, contracted what seemed to be the flu coupled with pneumonia. For three days she nursed him, giving him the best care known to medicine—quinine and mild stimulants. She massaged his weary limbs and kept him clean and comfortable in the hope that her nursing skills would bring him through. Tirelessly, she and the Tylees watched over their patient.

However, a problem with so many of the Indian patients was that they only came for help after they had been subjected to all kinds of unsanitary charms and superstitious cures by the village witch doctor. As an added pressure, Mildred and the Tylees knew they needed to save the patient, not only for the patient's sake, but for theirs as well. They knew the increasing influence they would have if their medicine and prayers proved stronger than the witchdoctor's. But regrettably, Manoel died on the third day. A heavy sorrow lay upon the missionaries. Mildred especially felt disheartened after so much effort and prayer on his behalf had been spent.

Reflecting on this experience, Arthur would write that from this death and sickness they learned much regarding the religious beliefs of the Nhambiquara and their standing with them. These indigenous people accused the missionaries of making them sick by the use of their medicines. But once they reminded the people of the many patients they had healed, they changed to saying that the death was caused by the evil spirit they called Thunder.

In any case, the Nhambiquara had now lost confidence in the missionaries. They picked up their deceased friend, tied him to the back of another, and then trekked forty miles through the jungle to their village. It would be three months before they would reappear at Juruena.

A Quick Death

The Nhambiquara returned to the mission station at the end of October. Neither the Tylees nor Mildred suspected treachery, which had been planned in the intervening time by the jealous village witchdoctor. On the morning of November 3, as Mildred was finishing breakfast with the Tylees, the murderous nightmare began.

As Mildred rose unsuspectingly from the table, all became a chaotic melee. At a given signal, a throng of Nhambiquara rushed into the house. One grabbed Mildred from behind, holding her in an armlock. Ethel leaped to her friend's aid, only to be pinned herself by another man. As Mildred stood in the clutches of her attacker, a poisonous arrow found its mark, sinking deep into her chest. Mildred keeled over on the floor and, as the poison took its effect, died from the fatal wound. In a matter of moments, five others died as well.

Crowns That Shall Be Theirs

Mildred's family was shocked at the word of the massacre. The news of her death was withheld as long as possible from her aging mother, as she was considered too weak to bear it. Memorial services were held, remembering the nurse who for so long had wanted to be a missionary.

Perhaps Mildred's brother, the Reverend Ronald Kratz, pastor of Western Springs Baptist Church, Illinois, best summed up what could be said about the massacre and the death of his sister:

> We are rejoicing in sorrow, rejoicing in the certainty of the resurrection, the blessed hope, and the crowns which shall be theirs.[2]

1. Moody Bible Institute Academic Records, Mildred Kratz.
2. Ronald Kratz, personal letter to Reverend Kenneth MacKenzie.

Born: April 12, 1894, Sigmaringen, Germany

Nationality: German

Attended Moody: 1928

Country of Service: Nicaragua

Mission: The Moravian Mission

Ministry: Church planter

Martyrdom: 1931, age 37, Musawas

Karl Bregenzer

"Somehow His name will be glorified"

Of all the martyrs of Moody, none are more controversial than Karl Bregenzer. Controversy not only surrounds the event of his death, but there are strong differences of opinion concerning his life and work as a missionary as well. Some view him as a self-giving servant of God and esteemed martyr, who fearlessly stood before Sandinista rebels proclaiming the gospel until the moment a machete severed his head from his body. Others saw him as a troublemaker who should have been sent home long before that fateful confrontation with the rebels took place.

Some mission records portray him as headstrong, tactless, and difficult to get along with. Further, it appears the home board covered up details of the events leading up to and of his death so that the particulars remain unknown even today. It also seems strange that very little tribute was paid this man who boldly made the ultimate sacrifice through his Christian witness. In addition, it is even questionable whether he should be claimed as a Moody martyr, since he spent so little time—six weeks—studying at the school.

Whatever one's opinion on Karl Bregenzer may be, it should be remembered that he lived and ministered in a danger-wracked country at a time when tensions were high. Political turmoil and civil unrest were rampant. Add to the local situation the unwanted intrusion of United States Marines, which sparked much anti-American sentiment, and it becomes clear that Karl and his family were caught in the midst of a situation that completely taxed their calling. It seems that Karl Bregenzer's story is a story of what can happen when, as a foreigner, a missionary does not remain neutral in a politically explosive situation.

Early Years

Karl was born on April 12, 1894, to Roman Catholic parents in Sigmaringen, Germany. Growing up, Karl was a restless and adventuresome young man. At seventeen, he immigrated to America by himself. The next seven years of his life were spent working on banana ships sailing between Texas and Central America and herding sheep in Texas. In 1918 while visiting a German family in Wisconsin, he met and later married Elizabeth Remke. Elizabeth, a bookkeeper, was a Moravian, and soon Karl was genuinely converted to Christ and became a Moravian himself.

A changed man, he now had a desire to study more deeply his newfound faith. To his credit, he took concrete steps to do just that. He and Elizabeth moved to Bethlehem, Pennsylvania, where he entered Moravian Theological Seminary. Following graduation in 1922, he was ordained a deacon in the church. While in seminary Karl was deeply moved by the pamphlet *Hallelujah and the Tom Toms*, written by missionary Samuel Wedman. The urgent appeal for missionaries from that booklet led Karl, Elizabeth, and Elizabeth's mother, Mrs. Remke, to Nicaragua under The Moravian Mission (now the Moravian Church in North America, Board of World Missions).

First Years in Nicaragua

Karl, Elizabeth, and Mrs. Remke arrived in Nicaragua in 1922. The three labored at Karawala, a mission station just inland from the Atlantic Ocean on the Rio Grande River. Although Karl's ministry was characterized by fervent evangelism, from correspondence it is clear he was a maverick and troublemaker. However, the exact nature and extent of his offenses are not clear. Two years into his term he was asked to agree to follow the church's rules or be dismissed. The following year, for an unknown reason, he was forcibly removed from a church.

The next year a fellow missionary asked the bishop to recall Karl back to the States because of his obstinate spirit and so that he could not pose as a "martyr." It is not clear what he was doing that caused the board to fear he was unnecessarily posing as a martyr, but it was something the mission was not taking lightly. Meanwhile, Elizabeth became quite ill and was on the verge of a breakdown. In 1927 Karl took his family back to Wisconsin for a much needed rest and to allow Elizabeth to recuperate.

During the years that the Bregenzers were at Karawala, two events were happening elsewhere in the country that would affect their future. One was the turning of a whole tribe en masse to the gospel—the Sumu people farther inland at a place called Musawas turned to Christ in a united people movement. Upon hearing of this event, another Moravian missionary went to the area and baptized over two hundred converts. He left behind a Karawala believer as the village evangelist.

Politically at this time there was the rise of the violent revolutionary General Augusto Cesar Sandino. Sandino and his rebels were bent on taking over the country by force and ending the American occupation. His followers were known as the Sandinistas, who in time became known for their cruel guerrilla warfare tactics.

Back in the States

Meanwhile, the Bregenzers had returned to Watertown, Wisconsin. Once there they set up home and got the family settled. By now they had two small children: Karl Junior and Ruth. Sensing Karl's need for spiritual refreshment, a friend offered to pay his expenses if he would attend Moody Bible Institute for a term of study. Karl took him up on the offer and went to Moody in January 1928. Since he wanted to return to Nicaragua in March, he only had time for a brief six-week half term. He left Moody in the dead of winter, picked up his family, and boarded a ship to Nicaragua.

A New Start

Upon their return to Nicaragua, the mission asked the Bregenzers to open up a permanent work among the newly evangelized Sumu people at Musawas. Karl and Elizabeth were delighted to become the first resident missionaries to this responsive tribe. Getting to the distant Musawas from the port city of Bluefields became a difficult proposition. The rebel Sandino was still at large, and the United States Marines had requisitioned all available boats in their efforts to capture him and his followers. Finally, after months of waiting, the Bregenzers were able to charter a boat that took them most the way.

After two months in transit they finally reached Musawas in October. As the three-boat caravan was docking, the villagers lined up on the banks singing in Miskito, "Sing them over again to me, wonderful words of life!" It was apparent that the resident national evangelist had done his job well and that the missionaries were welcomed to the village. The Bregenzers committed themselves to the work. Their first two years proved to be quite successful. They were able to build a church, hold services, start a school, and tend to medical needs.

Encounter with the Sandinistas

In time the Bregenzers discovered that one of their main helpers, who claimed he was a former witch doctor, was continuing to practice his craft. Painfully, Karl found it necessary to excommunicate him from church membership. The offended brother retaliated by stirring up a great deal of trouble for Karl, persuading a good number of people to his side.

At the same time the Bregenzers and the villagers were becoming alarmed by the insurgence of more and more rebels into the area. For survival tactics, the Bregenzers practiced contingency drills of hiding food, clothes, and themselves in the jungle. By February 1931 the threat was so real, they spent several days hiding in the jungle until a rebel threat had passed.

In the midst of this unrest, Karl made efforts to continue carrying on the work. Although it cannot be fully verified, some believe that Karl was also sending information about rebel activity to the American manager at a nearby mine. Also, even though he was a German citizen, it appears he did offer his services to the United States Marines as an informant. Meanwhile, the vengeful excommunicated witch doctor made contact with the rebels, telling them they would do the village a big favor by killing the missionary.

On March 31 Pedro Balandon, a general in Sandino's army, entered the village with a band of marauding men. An alarm was sounded on the far end of the village. Karl dropped what he was doing and, following the drill, got his two children, mother-in-law, and Elizabeth out of the village in advance of the rebels. Following the pre-practiced drills, they had time to reach their jungle hideaway. Just before she left, Elizabeth pleaded with Karl to join them, but putting a New Testament into his pocket he replied, "No, my place is here. They won't do so much damage to the property if I am present, and it will also give me opportunity to give them the gospel. If it be His will that they kill me, then I know that somehow His name will be glorified, and that is all that is important!" Elizabeth left and, turning at the jungle's edge for a last look, saw her husband, bravely waving a farewell. Ten minutes later he was a prisoner of the Sandinistas.

What happened next can only be reconstructed by the accounts of some of the remaining villagers. One report says the rebels tied his hands together and dragged him around the village, kicking and pummeling him. Another states that he stood in their midst and with his one free hand held out the Spanish New Testament, from which he read as he addressed his captors.

Whatever the case, the impatient Balandon was ready to see Karl dead. He put a machete in the hands of a villager loyal to Bregenzer and commanded him to kill the missionary. The man shouted that he would not and quickly scurried into the jungle ahead of gunshots. He was able to find Elizabeth and the rest of the family and told them what had happened. Back in the village, Balandon next commanded one of his own men to kill Bregenzer. The executioner took the machete and in one quick swipe severed the missionary's head from his body. Karl keeled over dead. Some rebels dug a shallow grave and threw his body into it. Others searched the surrounding jungle for his family, but to no avail. They were safely hidden in their hideout. Karl had saved his family, not only by staying in the village and distracting the rebels, but also by the contingency drills he had put them through.

However, the Sandinistas were not finished yet. Mockingly, they amused themselves by lounging around in the Bregenzer's house, listening to the family's record player while they giddily ate and drank what remained. After a while they departed, torching the house and church and destroying most of the village on their way out.

The Rosewood Cross

It was a year before the native Christians felt that it was safe to return to their village. One of the first things they did was to exhume the shallow grave of their beloved missionary and give him a proper burial. A short while later the Moravian Bishop Guido Grossmann came to Musawas to pay tribute to the slain missionary. He erected a cross on the spot where Karl had been murdered. The cross was made from the same piece of rosewood that Karl had been holding

the moment the alarm had been sounded. On Karl's grave he placed
a stone with the words

"For I am not ashamed of the gospel of Christ;
for it is the power of God unto salvation to every
one that believeth."

Born: November 28, 1922, Azalia, Indiana

Nationality: American

Graduated from Moody: 1956

Country of Service: Mexico

Mission: Air Mail From God

Ministry: Pilot

Martyrdom: 1956, age 33, Paraje Las Pintas, San Bartono, Morelos

Ancel Edwin Allen

"Why This Waste?"

Ancel stood stunned as he listened to the news coming from the Moody hangar radio. Five missionaries, down in the jungles of Ecuador, had not been heard from. It seemed they might have been killed by a small band of Auca Indians they were trying to reach with the gospel. Nate Saint, Jim Elliot, Roger Youderian, Ed McCully, and Peter Fleming were all missing and feared dead, but the remoteness of the location made it unclear. It was January 1956.

A few days later Ancel, along with his Moody shop mates, soberly listened to the update as the drama reached a climax. The suspicion of tragedy in the jungle was confirmed as a search-and-rescue party had finally reached a tiny sandbar on a remote river. The missionaries had named the stretch "palm beach," using it as a base camp to reach the obscure and elusive Auca Indians. The spear-pierced bodies of the five were discovered along with the torn wreckage of the small mission plane that had flown them in. News of the discovery sent shock waves throughout North American churches and beyond. The secular media grabbed hold of the story, giving it international exposure. *Life* magazine printed graphic pictures of the death scene, helping the world to visualize what had taken place. One newspaper questioned the tragedy of losing five bright, promising missionaries with the headline "Why This Waste?"

Ancel was determined not to let the death of these five young men be a waste. The brutal killing of these missionary pioneers made a profound impact on him. He told his wife, Naomi, that he was all the more determined to use his skills as a pilot and mechanic to take the gospel to those who had not yet heard. Like many in every corner of the world who heard the tragic story of "Operation Auca," Ancel rededicated his life to service for God. He determined to zealously serve his Lord as soon as possible after graduation. He had just five months of training left before he would be available to go and serve.

Pre-Moody Years

Ancel Edwin Allen was born in the tiny town of Azalia, Indiana, on November 28, 1922. Although raised in a home that had Christian influence, he did not know as he was growing up what a personal relationship with Christ really was. His childhood and teenage years were spent as a typical young person, except that he loved and had a knack for electronic gadgets. He would spend his days tinkering with radios, phonographs, and whatever else electronic he could get his hands on.

Then World War II erupted. As a twenty-one-year-old high school graduate, Ancel entered military service in 1943. Enlisting in the United States Air Force, he was sent through the service's radio school and then shipped out to the Pacific. Ancel spent the rest of the war doing his part as a radio technician on several different islands as the allies made their advance against the Japanese. Although he was not born again at the time, like so many service men, encountering different peoples and cultures had an effect upon him. The war was finally won in August of 1945. Five months after VJ Day he was discharged and returned to his hometown in central Indiana.

Over the next seven years, Ancel worked at a variety of jobs. Capitalizing on the training he received in the air force, he started as a radio technician. But with the advent of television, he switched to become a TV troubleshooter and repairman with RCA. He also operated an airport with two partners for a while, during which time he obtained his private pilot license. It was at this time that a twenty-one-year-old named Naomi entered his life. Ancel was seven years her senior, and the two fell in love.

In the fall of 1950 two events occurred that changed him forever. First, and most important, Ancel turned his life over to Christ and took Him as his personal Savior. Two months later he took Naomi to be his wife. As a new husband and a new believer, his desire was to follow God's will for his life. Reading books such as *George Mueller of Bristol* taught him what a life of faith was like. He wanted to live that kind of life. Reflecting on his time in the Pacific and remembering the lost groups of peoples he had encountered, he felt God leading him to take the gospel to those who had not yet had an opportunity to believe. Naomi heartily agreed.

Moody Training

Acting on this new commitment, Ancel quit his job with RCA and entered Moody's Missionary Technical Course in the fall of 1953. At the time the school was located twenty miles west of the main campus at the Wood Dale Airport.[1] So, from Gosport, Indiana, it was off to Chicago for Ancel and Naomi. Naomi took advantage of the day-school program for two years while Ancel earned his airframe/power-plant license and commercial and flight instructor ratings. Ancel also proved himself capable in "people" ministry as well. It was said of him, "One of the very best Sunday school teachers at the Bible Witness Mission. A fine group member and leader."[2]

During his final semester, Ancel met Nyles G. Huffman, the director of a small mission called Air Mail From God that flew in Mexico. Huffman, a pilot, was looking for another to join him in the newly established work. Feeling led to join this fledging work, Ancel and Naomi signed up. A few weeks later in June, Ancel graduated from Moody eager to go.

Martyrdom within a Month

Following graduation Ancel and Naomi returned briefly to Indiana to say good-bye to family and friends. Itching to get started on their mission, they left soon afterward. First they traveled to California where the Air Mail From God headquarters was located for a brief orientation. By mid-August they arrived in Toluca, Mexico, located just west of Mexico City. Here they settled in and set up base from which Ancel would do his flying.

Air Mail From God had a unique strategy of using airplanes for getting the gospel into the hands of villagers. First, the pilot flew low over a village, buzzing the houses to get people's attention. He would then turn and do a return run, dropping copies of the gospel of John on the villagers below. Each gospel of John had an application attached to it for interested people to use to sign up for a correspondence course. Later, Christian workers would follow up on the village, seeking out those who expressed interest in the gospel message and the course offered.

Ancel zealously began flying as many runs a day as possible, showering gospels of John on a multitude of villages. At a record-breaking pace he kept flying flight after flight. Many times Naomi would sit in the seat behind him, shoving the literature out the door as Ancel buzzed the villages. During the first five weeks they dropped an astounding fifty-five thousand gospels.[3]

However, not everyone on the ground below was happy with the showers of paper that were falling on them. Indeed, some thought it quite rude that this Protestant gringo would use such an annoying tactic to influence them to turn from their long-held beliefs. Something had to be done, and in late September some took action.

On the morning of September 21, just over a month after Ancel had begun his flights, he took to the sky to resume his literature-

dropping runs to the north. He could not know that mischief awaited
him below. As he flew over the village of San Bartono, Morelos, gunmen were waiting. When his plane came within range, they opened
fire, pummeling the craft with bullets. The shooting was lethal. A couple of the bullets from a high-powered rifle had ripped through the
plane and pierced his body.

Ancel's plane did a nosedive, crashing to the ground a short distance away. Villagers running to the crash site found 6,500 gospel
booklets that had burst forth from the ruptured hull. They also discovered Ancel's lifeless body in the cockpit. The gunmen probably
knew what Ancel knew—that the town would have never been the
same had the gospels been distributed to its people.

The official death certificate written up by the Mexican authorities put the crash at 10:30 a.m. In an apparent cover-up, it mentions
nothing about the cause of the crash, only that it happened and that
Ancel had died of "traumatic shock with profound contusion of the
thorax."[4] The follow-up mission report was quite different: "The
attackers had tried to hammer over the bullet holes in the fuselage
without success. They had also tried to dig the bullets from his body
with a knife in an effort to disguise the cause of death."[5]

Mexican believers helped Naomi bury Ancel the following day at
the general cemetery. In her grief, Naomi was greatly encouraged by
those whose lives had been transformed by the gospel. She was not
bitter, but simply wrote that the people who shot Ancel down did so
because they had yet to understand the Word, which he was trying
to give them.

End to a Mission

From a human standpoint, this abrupt end to a zealous life seemed
to be a total defeat. Mexican authorities never charged anyone with

the crime. Two years later Huffman, the mission's director, experienced the identical fate. Another mission eventually absorbed Air Mail From God, and its name and the records of its accomplishments were lost to time. Only eternity will tell what impact was made by the briefest of service—five weeks—of this Moody martyr.

Waste and Grace

"Why this waste?" became the first question people naturally asked when Ancel and the others whose stories have been recounted in this book lost their lives in Christian service. Why would highly trained, dedicated, talented people put themselves on foreign soil, knowing all too well that their futures could well be "thrown away" by acts of violence against them? Was this senseless, irresponsible behavior on their parts?

The only feasible explanation can be summed up in one short word—GRACE.

Each one of these men and women experienced the saving grace of God in their lives. This grace had such impact on their lives that they wanted others to experience that same sovereign grace as well . . . no matter how geographically, culturally, or religiously distant these people might be. No matter what the cost might have been personally to them, they did not consider their efforts spent seeking lost souls as a "waste." Rather, they viewed their lives as channels of life-giving grace.

It was the good news of God's wonderful grace that drove them to proclaim it to others living in distant parts of the globe. In the process of transmitting that life-changing message, God granted to each of them one of the noblest expressions of His care—A Martyr's Grace.

1. Gene A. Getz, *MBI—The Story of Moody Bible Institute*, 108.
2. Moody Bible Institute Academic Records, Ancel Allen.
3. James and Marti Hefley, *By Their Blood*, 567.
4. Death Certificate
5. James and Marti Hefley, Ibid.

Grace Abounding

II Corinthians 9:8
adapted by M.J.N.

Marvin J. Newell

1. In the struggle of my day, doubt, de-feat will plague my way, If
2. God is a-ble to make all grace a-bound when-e'er I call, Suff-
3. When— op-po-si-tion brings per-se-cu-tion, suf-fer-ing, Sus-

on my strength, my might, my pow'r re-ly._____ But God's sov-ereign grace is
fi-cient in all things, all times, all ways._____ In His work I can a-
taining grace He gives me to en-dure._____ If____ called by Him to

strong, keeps my heart from do-ing wrong, Keeps me sure, helps me en-dure____ come what
bound, do His will wher-e-ver found, Led by grace, at His____ pace I car-ry
die, my heart trem-bles deep in-side, Mar-tyr's grace, in its____ place He will pro-

may._____   Grace a-bound-ing,_____ rich and free,_____
on._____
vide._____

Grace a - bound-ing _____ a - bun-dant - ly. _____ Grace

bound-ing, _____ in time of need, _____ Grace a -

bound - ing for you and me. _____

©2006

Putting Martyrdom in Perspective

Since reflections on martyrdom cannot be passed along by those who have personally experienced it, it is up to the living to be observers in an effort to bring understanding to the topic. Yet, just as spectators sitting in the bleachers of a sporting event can never fully fathom the full measure of what players on the field are experiencing, so writers on this topic can only deliver secondhand what they cognitively gather as inquisitive bystanders. For most who make the attempt, it is done at a safe distance.

Yet, the premature death of a follower of Christ as a result of human hostility has an enduring impact on observant believers. It causes most to pause and ponder anew the extreme cost of discipleship. It forces many to question whether they themselves measure up to the highest standard of devotion to Christ and His cause. It motivates still others to abandon selfish plans and ambitions and turn to serve Christ in hard and difficult places. It creates a baseline for the church from which to measure its worth—whether its activities are meaningful and truly important in light of eternity.

Martyrdom has its value.

Why This Study from Moody

Other Bible schools and seminaries could provide a book similar to this. Why a book on martyrs from Moody Bible Institute? It certainly was not because Moody has a corner on the subject, and not necessarily because it has the most graduates who have been martyred while serving as missionaries. Rather, one reason is the rich mission history that is associated with the school. Throughout its 130 years of existence, thousands of graduates have served in dangerous and volatile places around the globe. One hundred and four years of mission history (1898–2002) is covered in this reflection.

Through those years Moody martyrs were put to death in a vast array of historical settings. From the little-known "Hut Tax War" in Sierra Leone (1898), to the Boxer Rebellion in China (1900); through the bloody years of unsettled China and congruently the pioneering efforts in the Amazon basin in the 1930s; right through World War II, to the Vietnam War and Simba Rebellion of the 1960s; to present-day unrest in the Middle East, Moody has experienced its fair share of martyrs—twenty-one to be exact.

Against an array of historical backdrops, the typical variety of ministries missionaries were involved in throughout the past century are portrayed. Moody missionary martyrs were serving as bush pilots, Bible translators, medical doctors, nurses, teachers, professors, social workers, pioneer church planters, and field administrators. While performing ordinary mission tasks, they were ordinary people who became caught up in extraordinary situations.

Place of Martyrdom in Persecution

Not all persecution is equally intense or carries equal consequences. Believers experience various degrees of persecution, with martyrdom experienced as the final degree. In Matthew 10, for the first time Jesus commissioned His disciples for a mission. Before sending them out, He explicitly cautioned them that they would face varying degrees of opposition. His lesson to them can serve as a template for all missionaries of all ages.

Six phrases are used by Jesus to describe six increasingly intense hostilities that opposition can take. He begins with the least severe form, progressing in ascending order to the ultimate human hostility —martyrdom. In this lesson Christ shows that His messengers could expect to be: prevented, "does not receive you" (v. 14); rejected, "nor heed your words" (v. 14); detained, "deliver you up" (vv. 17, 19, KJV); physically abused, "scourge you" (v. 17, KJV); pursued with intent to harm, "persecute you" (v. 23); and finally martyred, "kill the body" (v. 28). It is instructive to note that Jesus declared that opposition would come from the state (v. 18), religious leaders (v. 17), or family members (v. 21). Losing one's life as a result of human hostility in a situation of witness is the ultimate persecution experience.

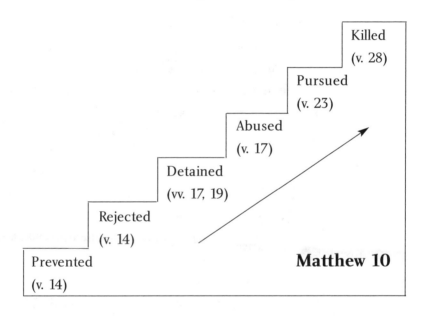

Lessons Learned from the Martyrs

1. There seems to be no specific personal qualification for one to enter the ranks of martyrdom.

> While these men and women were students in training at Moody, none of them planned or expected to die as a martyr. Martyrdom is not something a person anticipates or to which one readily aspires. It is a trial that God in His providence

bestows on select individuals for purposes ultimately known only to Him. He is not capricious in a matter as heart wrenching as this. God's selection of those who so die may appear arbitrary at times. However, we can say with confidence that His plans are sure and purposeful in each one of these deaths. The truth of Romans 8:28–30 gives perspective in this regard.

2. Great gains are realized in martyrdom.

Paul states that for the believer "to die is gain" (Philippians 1:21). Gains at death are especially true for the Christian martyr. Over and over stories recount gains that are achieved when the life of a servant of God is taken on account of Him. Gains achieved in martyrdom are best understood from three perspectives.

Gains in relation to the martyr: Ultimately the martyr whose life has been sacrificed has reached a glorious new existence! The martyr is now in the untainted glorious presence of His Master, where "fullness of joy" and eternal pleasures abound (Psalm 16:11). That person now has become and enjoys all that God had intended for mankind from the very beginning. Unimagined benefits are experienced. But beyond that, martyrs rightfully receive a special recognition that will be noticed by all throughout eternity. A "crown of life" is a special emblem of honor, rewarding them for faithfulness until death (Revelation 2:10).

Gains in relation to the work: As seen in these accounts, many times ministries initially experience a setback and even devastating loss immediately following the death of a martyr. Besides life being taken, property often is destroyed, followers scattered, and the work left in disarray. However, once the impact of the death is felt around the broader Christian community, it is not long before greater gains are realized. In most instances, more funds are given, more initiatives are started, and more volunteers come forward as the impact of the martyr's death makes its mark. Following the Boxer Rebellion in 1900, when two Moody graduates died, the number of Protestants in China more than doubled over the following six years. Powerful soul-cleansing revivals surged across North China, and wave after wave of new missionaries along with millions of dollars for evangelization and education were sent from the West.[1] Over and over this same kind of response has been repeated where martyr blood has been spilt.

Gains in relation to God: God always gains when His followers lay down their lives for Him. Satan attempts to make God look bad, weak, and defeated by those deaths. But God has His way of showing otherwise. God gains by showing the world the cost of the cross—demonstrating anew through His martyrs the suffering of Christ Himself. He gains when Christians so moved by the martyr's example rededicate themselves to Him and to His cause. He gains when ministries expand, bringing forth crops of new believers. But more preciously, He gains when His beloved martyr is welcomed into His presence to enjoy Him forever. "Precious in the sight of God is the death of his saints" (Psalm 116:15, KJV) is especially true when God welcomes home one whose life was taken because of His cause.

3. Much pain is experienced in martyrdom.

We tend to romanticize the experience of martyrdom, believing that there is nothing but triumphant victory derived from the experience. The reality of the matter is that there is a flip side to be soberly considered as well: pain and loss.

Pain in relation to the martyr: To lose one's life prematurely by human hostile action is in every instance a physically painful experience. Moody martyrs were beheaded, stabbed, choked, shot, speared, and stoned. There are times when martyr deaths are so glamorized that the gruesomeness is too often minimized. We need to be reminded that these people suffered pain as they spilled their blood. Some, as they went through a prolonged death experience, were traumatized through the course of it. Betty Stam, for example, witnessed the beheading of her husband before her own. Ella Schenck and Hulda Jane Stumpf were terribly mistreated before their deaths. Others, such as Bonnie Witherall, were taken quite suddenly, with but an instant of suffering. All experienced painful deaths.

Pain in relation to loved ones left behind: Wives, husbands, children, and extended family members forever feel the pain of losing their martyred loved one. Some do recover from the ordeal and use it as a means of grace and growth. Others do not and for life bear the scars, heartache, and consequences of having their beloved taken. Baby Helen Stam was forced to grow up incognito and with a changed name in order to avoid unwanted popularity that the death of her parents brought. It was discovered in interviews with surviving spouses of other recent Moody martyrs that some of their children have not fared well since the death of their parent. Disillusionment, deep spiritual struggles, broken marriages, and heartache plague many surviving family members, especially children.

4. A special "grace" seems to be extended to martyrs.

> For those martyrs who have time to contemplate what is happening and see their death coming, God seems to grant a special "grace" to endure the impending ordeal. In many cases God grants a surreal, tranquil spirit, a serenity of heart and mind that transcends understanding. That spirit of peace leads to a genuine surrender that is derived from an overarching eternal perspective on life. An unshakable faith in something better in store for them helped many martyrs to calmly bear their trial.

> When D. L. Moody was asked if he could endure a martyr's death, he replied that God would at that moment grant a "martyr's grace." Several of the Moody martyrs exhibited that kind of grace. In the instance of the Stams, although there is no written record, they exhibited a martyr's grace by their example of humble surrender as they knelt to take the executioner's sword. Mary Baker, held captive by the Simba rebels and awaiting her death, could say, "With me, it was settled long ago, 'by life or by death' and there it rests!" As Esther Nordlund in central China stood next to the bodies of her two slain colleagues, she could calmly say to her executors, "Yes, you may kill me too." Almost fifty years earlier in that same country during the Boxer Rebellion, Mrs. E. R. Atwater of the China Inland Mission in her final letter written after two months of suspense would write:

> > I am preparing for the end very quietly and calmly. The Lord is wonderfully near, and He will not fail me. I was very restless and excited while there seemed a chance of life, but God has taken away that feeling,

and now I just pray for grace to meet the terrible end bravely. . . . I cannot imagine the Savior's welcome.[2]

Her letter epitomizes a martyr's grace granted by God in time of need that appears to be the experience of most.

5. In martyrdom, "justice" is never served.

In no instance in the deaths of the twenty-one Moody martyrs was one perpetrator of the martyr's death was ever brought to justice. Actually none was ever apprehended and therefore was neither jailed, tried, convicted, nor punished for the crime. Perhaps this is what qualifies their deaths as martyrdom—that the sacrifice is accepted as a nonpunitive crime. After all, these individuals were proclaiming Jesus, the ultimate Forgiver, who at the event of His own death could plead, "Father, forgive them, for they know not what they do." The highest priority of missions is to engage the lost by proclaiming a forgiving Jesus, not to seek justice. Ultimately, in His time and in His way, it will be God who avenges the blood of His martyrs:

> When he opened the fifth seal, I saw under the altar the souls of those who had been slain because of the word of God and the testimony they had maintained. They called out in a loud voice, "How long, Sovereign Lord, holy and true, until you judge the inhabitants of the earth and avenge our blood?" Then each of them was given a white robe, and they were told to wait a little longer, until the number of their fellow servants and brothers who were to be killed as they had been was completed."   —Revelation 6:9–12, NIV

6. Seeking after martyrdom is unchristian.

> Martyrs' motives need examination. In a day of rampant sui-
> cide bombers who glorify and justify the destruction of inno-
> cent lives as an act of martyrdom, it is right to question
> motives. It can be categorically demonstrated from Scripture
> that for one to seek after martyrdom is a very unchristian
> thing to do. The intentional destruction of one's own life, by
> putting oneself in harm's way with the intent of being killed,
> cloaked in excuse that it is for the cause of Christ, is selfish,
> self-serving, and sinful. Those who would attempt this course
> of action are out for self-glory to make a name for themselves.
> It is their hope that others would applaud them for their
> action and thus bring a degree of admiration to themselves
> that they could not achieve otherwise.
>
> Every instance of martyrdom in Scripture and in the history
> of Moody is just the opposite. Rather than self-seeking, men
> and women were self-abasing as they served in the work of
> God when their lives were taken. They stood boldly, but not
> recklessly, for Christ when called to do so. Rather than real-
> izing a name for themselves, they realized the glorification of
> God through their sacrifice. That is why so many were forgot-
> ten. Rather than intentionally putting themselves in harm's
> way, they were caught, dragged, and forced to the place of
> harm. Rather than elevated as heroes and heroines, most
> martyrs of Moody were relegated to the annals of obscurity.
>
> This is why we must stand in sharp disagreement with those
> who suggest that "martyrdom is in essence a type of 'glorified
> suicide.'"[3] These writers go on to state, "It is not always easy
> to distinguish between 'suicide' and 'martyrdom,' between
> killing oneself and provoking one's own death."[4]

To not be able to distinguish between the two is an intentional attempt to distort what the two experiences really are. A person who stands firm for what she believes, especially in religious beliefs, is not attempting to provoke her own death. No person begs to be killed simply for defending a faith position or because she is engaged in a religious profession. That would be self-defeating and defeating to the cause itself. In essence these statements by Droge and Tabor seem to make the martyr responsible for the murderer's action, when in fact the one doing the killing needs to be held responsible for his own aggressive behavior.

7. The martyr cannot be dishonored.

Martyrs for the cause of Christ are appropriately given their due share of respect. Instead of being discredited, they are immortalized. One reason this book was written was to resurrect the memory and bring honor to those whose lives and deaths brought glory to Christ through their ultimate sacrifice. But that goal was not to be an end in and of itself. Rather, the higher goal was to use these stories to encourage Christian workers in dangerous areas and hard places to continue to persevere in their callings, even though they are serving in life-threatening situations. To honor martyrs for providing this incentive is the right thing to do.

Over 160 years ago, Ralph Waldo Emerson wrote about "compensation" in this regard. He stated that the history of persecution is a history of endeavors to cheat the natural order of things. Throughout the history of the church, those who took a martyr's life always thought they were discrediting both the person and the cause for which he was killed. However, to the contrary, the opposite became true. Emerson insightfully stated:

> The martyr cannot be dishonored. Every lash inflicted is a tongue of fame; every prison a more illustrious abode; every burned book or house enlightens the world; every suppressed or expunged word reverberates through the earth from side to side. The minds of men are at last aroused, reason looks out and justifies her own, and malice finds all her work in vain. It is the whipper who is whipped and the tyrant who is undone.[5]

In this same vein, Martin Luther, writing centuries before of the murder of George Winkler by the Bishop of Mainz, said much the same:

> Therefore will I translate the cry of his blood from the earth, that such a murder may nevermore be silent until God shall execute vengeance on Satan who brought the deed, so that instead of one murdered George, a hundred other true-hearted preachers may arise who shall do Satan a thousand-fold more harm than this one man has done.[6]

Ever since the crucifixion of Christ, it has been common for the Christian martyr to be jeered, ridiculed, mocked, scorned, lambasted, and shamed as his or her life is being taken. This strategy is employed by the killers to make the martyr feel useless, worthless, and wrong and to make the death seem senseless and useless. However, we know that in truth for the cause of Christ these martyrs can never be dishonored.

8. Martyrdom as a strategy of evangelism

> Karen White, in the EMS series article "Overcoming Resistance through Martyrdom," has stated that it is a revolutionary thought that martyrdom might be an intentional strategy of God to bring the world to Himself.[7] A couple of decades ago a major mission strategy was to take the gospel to the least resistant peoples of "ripe" fields. In recent years the strategy has been flip-flopped. The focus is now on reaching the least reached peoples found mostly in resistant places. White suggests that we can expect more missionary martyrs as staunchly held Muslim, Hindu, and Buddhist areas are penetrated.

> White reminds us that martyrdom has two sides to it. One is what humans do to God's servants. The other is what God intends to accomplish through it.[8] No martyrdom is an accident. God is never caught off guard by the death of any of His servants. He has purposes and plans by the calling of some to die while in His service. It is for the advancement of world evangelization, not the curtailing of it.

> The cold-blooded murder of Bonnie Witherall in Lebanon is a prime example of God using a seemingly senseless and tragic death to further His evangelistic purposes. Rather than a decrease of student interest and recent recruits for the Middle East, there has been a surge of interest and commitment to that area. God has His ways of using martyrdom to advance His agenda.

9. Martyrdom as an example to local believers

> When compared to the number of missionaries who have gone overseas from Moody through the years, the number

that have been martyred is minuscule. Less than 1/100 of 1 percent have so died. In terms of raw statistics alone, it could be argued that the cost and effects have not been really that great. At least so it seems.

However, the impact of those deaths on local believers in the locales where those deaths took place is immeasurable. In many instances, not only has the work expanded and adherents increased, but the local followers have been emboldened in their resolve to remain loyal to Christ. Resolve on their part to bear up under persecution is enhanced. By example of the missionary martyr, local believers have a model to follow and a death to emulate as they in turn stand against the oppression that comes with their commitment to Christ. Many of them may die as martyrs too, and their deaths will be more numerous than the missionaries who brought the gospel to them. Reports from watch groups such as Voice of the Martyrs constantly remind us of this sober reality.

Conclusion

Though the martyrs themselves cannot personally present us with a missiological reflection on the topic, they do not remain silent. Indeed, even though they are gone, they speak to us from the grave. It becomes the responsibility of the living, then, to take pause and reflect on the heritage that has been passed along through their deaths. Only then will we be prepared to endure the same kind of treatment if so granted the honor (Philippians 1:29).

Let goods and kindred go, this moral life also;
the body they may kill; God's truth abideth still;
his kingdom is forever.

—Martin Luther, 1529, based on Psalm 46

1. James and Marti Hefley, *By Their Blood*, 44–46.
2. Taylor, *These Forty Years*.
3. Arthur J. Droge and James D. Tabor, *A Noble Death*, 2.
4. Ibid., 118.
5. Ralph Waldo Emerson, "Essays: Compensation," 2.
6. "Paoting Fu—Its Sad Memories," 117.
7. Karen L. White, "Overcoming Resistance through Martyrdom," 159.
8. Ibid., 168.

ACKNOWLEDGMENTS

No book that entails the research of historical events can be written without the help of others. Many individuals from a multitude of denominations, mission agencies, and schools throughout North America assisted me in gathering the materials needed to do the research behind these stories. In reconstructing what took place, this assistance helped to ensure the historical accuracy of these accounts, making them as true as possible to what transpired.

My heartfelt thanks go to the following: Joe Cataio, Archivist, Moody Bible Institute Archives; Robert D. Shuster and Wayne Weber, Archivists, Billy Graham Center Archives, Wheaton College; Betty Layton, Archivist, American Baptist Historical Society Archives Center; Gail Stevens Shouds, United Theological Seminary Archives and Center for the Evangelical United Brethren Heritage; Ralmon Jon Black, Secretary, Williamsburg Historical Society, Williamsburg, MA; Lillian Valle and Mark Shenise, General Board of Global Ministries, United Methodist Church; Dr. David Broucek, TEAM; Dr. Virgil Reeves, CrossWorld; Dr. Charles Davis, Africa Inland Mission; Sharon

Dotson, Evangelical Covenant World Mission; Rose Carleton, OMF International, Canada; Suzanne Henderson, Board of World Missions, Moravian Church; Mrs. Linda Ridgway-Thompson, CA; Brenda Evans, Trinity Western University Alumni Department; and Mrs. Karen Begley, North Vernon, Indiana.

And of course I thank my family, who have supported me through the process. Their enduring the reading of chapter drafts and giving of suggestions was of much help.

To my wife, Peggy, to whom this book is dedicated, I owe the most by far. Not only did she critically proofread the chapters before they went to the publisher, but her constant encouragement got me through to the end.

Marvin J. Newell
Elgin, Illinois
September 2006

Sources

Chapter 1: Bonnie Witherall

Chicago Tribune, "Slain U.S. Missionary Mourned in Lebanon." November 25, 2002.

Chicago Tribune, "For a Better World, Grads of Moody Bible Soldier On," April 20, 2003.

Moody Alumni Magazine, "Bonnie Witherall, Missionary to Lebanon," Spring 2003.

Moody Bible Institute Academic Records, Bonnie Penner Witherall.

Moody Student, "Missionary Bonnie Witherall, 31, Killed in Lebanon," December 10, 2002.

Witherall, Gary. *Total Abandon.* Wheaton: Tyndale House, 2005.

http://www.cwfa.org. Concerned Women for America. "American Missionary Killed in Muslim Country," by Tanya L. Green. November 26, 2002.

http://www.cnnw.com. Christian News Northwest. "Missionary from Vancouver Shot Dead in Lebanon." December 2002.

http://www.fisherofmen.net. Fisher of Men. "A Tribute to Bonnie Witherall,". by Gary Kernaghan. November 21, 2004.

http://www.connectionmagazine.org. Connection—the Good News Magazine. "Missionary's Murder Will Open Doors in Lebanon, Agency Says," by Allie Martin. January 2003.

http://www.nyack.edu/2004. Nyack News. "Gary Witherall: Call to Christ." February 14, 2003.

Chapter 2: Hattie J. Rice

Allison, Lon, ed. *John R. Mott—That the World May Believe*. Wheaton: EMIS, 2002.

Broomhall, Marshall, ed. *Martyred Missionaries of the China Inland Mission*. London: Mogan & Scott, 1901.

Dorsett, Lyle W. *A Passion for Souls: The Life of D. L. Moody*. Chicago: Moody, 1997.

Hefley, James, and Marti Hefley. *By Their Blood: Christian Martyrs of the Twentieth Century*. Grand Rapids: Baker, 1996.

Smith, H. G. "Letter of Recommendation," June 20, 1890.

Tan, Chester C. *The Boxer Catastrophe*. New York: Columbia University Press, 1955.

Taylor, F. Howard. *These Forty Years: A Short History of the China Inland Mission*. Philadelphia: Pepper Publishing, 1903.

Tiedemann, R. G. "Baptism of Fire: China's Christians and the Boxer Uprising of 1900." International Bulletin of Missionary Research, January 2000.

Chapter 3: Josephine Elizabeth Desmond

Broomhall, Marshall, ed. *Martyred Missionaries of the China Inland Mission*. London: Mogan & Scott, 1901.

http://www.bartleby.com/5/105.html. Emerson, Ralph Waldo. *Essays and English Traits*. "V. Compensation," 1841.

Hefley, James, and Marti Hefley. *By Their Blood: Christian Martyrs of the Twentieth Century*. Grand Rapids: Baker, 1996.

Moody Bible Institute Academic Records, Josephine Desmond.

Tan, Chester C. *The Boxer Catastrophe.* New York: Columbia University Press, 1955.

Taylor, F. Howard. *These Forty Years: A Short History of the China Inland Mission.* Philadelphia: Pepper Publishing, 1903.

Tiedemann, R. G. "Baptism of Fire: China's Christians and the Boxer Uprising of 1900." *International Bulletin of Missionary Research,* January 2000.

Watkins, R. Daniel. *An Encyclopedia of Compelling Quotations.* Peabody, MA: Hendrickson Publishers, Inc., 2001.

Chapter 4: Eleanor E. Chesnut, M.D.

Anderson, Gerald H., ed. *Biographical Dictionary of Christian Missions.* Grand Rapids: Eerdmans, 1999.

Moody Bible Institute Academic Records, Eleanor Chesnut.

Montgomery, Helen Barrett. *Western Women in Eastern Lands.* New York: The MacMillan Company, 1910.

Moreau, A. Scott, ed. *Evangelical Dictionary of World Missions.* Grand Rapids: Baker, 2000.

Speer, Robert E. *Servants of the King.* New York: Young People's Missionary Movement of the United States and Canada, 1909.

Tucker, Ruth A. *Guardians of the Great Commission.* Grand Rapids: Zondervan, 1988.

Park College Record. Letter of November 1905, No. 40.

Chapter 5: Robert Elias Blomdahl

Hefley, James, and Marti Hefley. *By Their Blood: Christian Martyrs of the Twentieth Century.* Grand Rapids: Baker, 1996.

Moody Bible Institute Academic Records, Robert Blomdahl.

"Moody Bible Institute Martyrs," unpublished document, no author, no date.

Oscarrson, Roland. E-mail correspondence from director of Swedish Alliance Mission International Department, March 8, 2005.

Chapter 6: Gustaf David Nathaniel Tornvall

Beckman, Thyra. "Missionary Wedding in China." *The Missionary Broadcaster,* first quarter, 1932.

Castle, William. "Official Communication from the Department of State." July 1, 1932.

Grauer, Rev. O.C., ed. *Fifty Wonderful Years.* Chicago: Soderlund Printing Service, 1940.

"Gustav Tornvall Killed by Soldiers." *The Missionary Broadcaster,* third quarter, 1932 (July, August, September).

Moody Bible Institute Academic Records, Gustaf Tornvall.

Moody Monthly, "Alumni Gleanings," October 1932.

Olsen, Othilie. "An Appreciation of Gustav Tornvall." *The Missionary Broadcaster,* Vol. III, fourth quarter, 1932.

_____. "More About Tornvall's Death." *The Evangelist,* November 1932.

Peterson, Earl R. "The Work in Pingliang Moving Forward." *The Missionary Broadcaster.* first quarter, 1931.

Todd, O. J. "Gustaf Tornvall—An Outstanding Missionary." *The Missionary Broadcaster,* Vol. IX, first quarter, 1933.

Tornvall, Gustav. "Pingliang" (station report). *The Missionary Broadcaster,* second quarter, 1931.

R. A. Brehm of the Scandinavian Alliance Mission to Mr. William M. Runyan of the Moody Bible Institute, September 6, 1932.

Chapter 7: John Cornelius Stam

English, E. Schuyler. *By Life and by Death: Excerpts and Lessons from the Diary of John C. Stam.* Grand Rapids: Zondervan, 1938.

Hefley, James, and Marti Hefley. *By Their Blood: Christian Martyrs of the Twentieth Century.* Grand Rapids: Baker, 1996.

Huizenga, Lee S. *John and Betty Stam—Martyrs.* Grand Rapids: Zondervan, 1935.

Moody Bible Institute Academic Records, John Stam.

Taylor, Mrs. Howard. *John and Betty Stam: A Story of Triumph.* Chicago: Moody, 1935.

_____. *The Triumph of John and Betty Stam.* Philadelphia: China Inland Mission, 1935.

Shaw, Thomas A., and Dwight A. Clough. *Amazing Faith.* Chicago: Moody, 2003.

White, Kathleen. *John and Betty Stam.* Minneapolis: Bethany House, 1989.

Chapter 8: Betty Alden Stam

English, E. Schuyler. *By Life and by Death: Excerpts and Lessons from the Diary of John C. Stam.* Grand Rapids: Zondervan, 1938.

Hefley, James, and Marti Hefley. *By Their Blood: Christian Martyrs of the Twentieth Century.* Grand Rapids: Baker, 1996.

Huizenga, Lee S. *John and Betty Stam—Martyrs.* Grand Rapids: Zondervan, 1935.

Moody Bible Institute Academic Records, Elizabeth Stam.

Taylor, Mrs. Howard. *John and Betty Stam: A Story of Triumph.* Chicago: Moody, 1935.

_____. *The Triumph of John and Betty Stam.* Philadelphia: China Inland Mission, 1935.

Shaw, Thomas A., and Dwight A. Clough. *Amazing Faith.* Chicago: Moody, 2003.

White, Kathleen. *John and Betty Stam.* Minneapolis: Bethany House, 1989.

Chapter 9: Esther Victoria Nordlund

Cervin, Russell A. *Covenant Missions in China/Taiwan.* Chicago: Department of World Mission Evangelical Covenant Church of America, 1970.

Dahlstrom, Earl C. "The Covenant Missionary Society in China." Doctorate thesis, Hartford Seminary Foundation, 1950.

Hefley, James, and Marti Hefley. *By Their Blood: Christian Martyrs of the Twentieth Century.* Grand Rapids: Baker, 1998.

Moody Bible Institute Academic Records, Esther Nordlund.

Wu, Liang Kazu. "The Lives and Martyrdom of China Missionaries Esther V. Nordlund, Martha J. Anderson, and Alexis F. Berg." *The Covenant Quarterly.* February 2003.

Chapter 10: Ella Mary Schenck

Anderson, Florence. "Bai Bureh: Warrior Hero." Mano Vision Newsletter, Issue 4, 1998.

Cox, Emmett D. *The Church of the United Brethren in Christ in Sierra Leone.* Pasadena: William Carey Library, 1970.

Fyfe, Christopher. *A History of Sierra Leone.* Oxford: Oxford University Press, 1962.

Hefley, James, and Marti Hefley. *By Their Blood: Christian Martyrs of the Twentieth Century.* Grand Rapids: Baker, 1998.

Kane, J. Herbert. *A Global View of Christian Missions.* Grand Rapids: Baker, 1971.

Latourette, Kenneth Scott. *A History of the Expansion of Christianity.*

Moody Bible Institute Academic Records, Ella Schenck.

Olson, Gilbert W. *Church Growth in Sierra Leone.* Grand Rapids: William Eerdmans, 1969.

Woman's Evangel XVII, no. 7, July 1898.

Chapter 11: Hulda Jane Stumpf

Dow, Philip. *School in the Clouds: The Rift Valley Academy Story.* Pasadena: William Carey Library, 2003.

Downing, Lee H. Letter to Rev. H. D. Campbell, January 10, 1930.

_____. Letter to Missionary Union of M.B.I., October 15, 1930.

East African Standard, "Martyred Missionary's Diary," Saturday, October 11, 1930.

Farewell words of Hulda Stumpf, "Inland Africa," no date.

"Gender & Women's Rights Book: Female Circumcision," March 2001, http://www.web.net/~iccaf/genderinfo/femalecirc0301.htm.

Hefley, James, and Marti Hefley. *By Their Blood: Christian Martyrs of the Twentieth Century.* Grand Rapids: Baker, 1998.

Inland Africa, XIV, no. 2, February, 1930.

_____ XIV, no. 5, May, 1930.

_____ XV, no. 1, January, 1931.

Barnet, Ted (president of Africa Inland Mission). 2003. Interview by Marvin Newell.

Moody Bible Institute Academic Records, Hulda Stumpf.

Official letter by H.W.E, to Mr. Harvey Walham, Mr. Ohwyn Ball Jr., and Mr. John L. Steele, dated January 4, 1930.

Stumpf, Hulda. "Farewell Words" in *Hearing and Doing,* Publication of Africa Inland Mission, April–June 1912.

Tucker, Ruth A. *From Jerusalem to Irian Jaya.* Grand Rapids: Zondervan, 2004.

Chapter 12: Lucia Hammond Cozzens

Moody Bible Institute Academic Records, Lucia Hammond.

Unpublished documents from the Presbyterian Historical Society:

Application, The Board of Foreign Missions of the Presbyterian Church in the U.S.A. Lucia Hammond, November 20, 1915.

"Day by day on a Trekking Trip," by Lucia Cozzens, October 8, 1927.

Memorial Minutes on Mrs. Edwin Cozzens, November 14–15, 1949.

Personal Record of Lucia Hammond Cozzens, September 26, 1934.

Personal summary of Mrs. Edwin Cozzens, revised, May 1948.

Preliminary Correspondence Blank of The Board of Foreign Missions of the Presbyterian Church in the U.S.A., filled out by Lucia Hammond, August 18, 1915.

Personal Record of Miss Lucia Hammond, January 31, 1922.

Personal file card: Cozzens, Mrs. Edwin (Lucia Hammond).

Chapter 13: Mary Elizabeth Baker

Baker, Mary. Personal letter, August 19, 1964.

Hayes, Margaret. *Captive of the Simbas.* New York: Harper & Row, 1966.

Hefley, James, and Marti Hefley. *By Their Blood: Christian Martyrs of the Twentieth Century.* 2nd ed. Grand Rapids: Baker, 1996.

Lifeline, quarterly of the Unevangelized Fields Mission, first quarter, 1966.

_____, fourth quarter, 1965.

Moody Bible Institute Academic Records, Mary Baker.

Chapter 14: Stanley Gordon Ridgway

Good News Magazine, "Once Again, UM Missionary Slain in Zaire," March/April 1985, pages 41–42.

Letter to General Board of Global Ministries—The United Methodist Church, November 20, 1984.

Mission Memo, "Zaire Missionary," December 1984.

Moody Bible Institute Academic Records, Stanley Ridgway.

New York Times, "Zaire Reports Retaking Town from Tanzania-Based Rebels," November 17, 1984.

Personal letter to Lowell Wertz (fellow pilot), November 20, 1984.

Personal letter to Pauline Chambers (eye witness), December 5, 1984.

UMC NEWS, November 19, 1984.

UMC NEWS, March 1986.

UMC NEWS, March 9, 1979.

United Methodist Reporter, "Missionary killed in Zaire," November 22, 1984.

Chapter 15: Erle Frederick Rounds

Adams, Jennie Clare. *The Hills Did Not Imprison Her.* New York: ABFMS, 1991. Poems written during the months from April 1942– December 1943.

Beaver, Raymond. "Partners in Mission: American Baptist and Philippine Baptist in Mission Together 1900–1985." Iloilo City: ABC Printing Center.

Hefley, James, and Marti Hefley. *By Their Blood: Christian Martyrs of the Twentieth Century.* Grand Rapids: Baker, 1996.

Moody Bible Institute Academic Records, Erle Rounds.

Missions (publication of American Baptist Church), "Missionary Martyrs in the Philippine Islands," 36, no. 7, September 1945.

Rounds, Erle. Personal Letter to the ABFMS board for appointment, October 24, 1929.

Spencer, Louise Reid. *Guerrilla Wife.* Chicago: Peoples Book Club, Inc., 1945.

Spencer, Louise Reid. "Guerilla Wife." *Ladies Home Journal,* August 1945.

Through Shining Archway. New York: American Baptist, June 1945.

Chapter 16: Signe Amelia Erickson

Adams, Jennie Clare. *The Hills Did Not Imprison Her.* New York: ABFMS, 1991. Poems written during the months from April 1942– December 1943.

Beaver, Raymond. "Partners in Mission: American Baptist and Philippine Baptist in Mission Together 1900–1985." Iloilo City: ABC Printing Center.

Hefley, James, and Marti Hefley. *By Their Blood: Christian Martyrs of the Twentieth Century.* Grand Rapids: Baker, 1996.

"In Memoriam." Unpublished document of American Baptist Foreign Mission Society, Woman's American Baptist Foreign Missionary Society. New York: May 1945.

Moody Bible Institute Academic Records, Signe Erikson.

"Miss Signe A. Erickson," appointment letter of American Baptist Foreign Mission Society, unpublished, no date.

Missions (publication of American Baptist Church), "Missionary Martyrs in the Philippine Islands," 36, no. 7, September 1945.

Personal letter by Signe Erickson, 1930.

Personal letter by Signe Erickson to Miss Hazel Shank, May 15, 1943. Written "somewhere in Free Panay, P.I."

Spencer, Louise Reid. *Guerrilla Wife.* Chicago: Peoples Book Club, Inc., 1945.

Spencer, Louise Reid. "Guerilla Wife." *Ladies Home Journal,* August 1945.

Through Shining Archway. New York: American Baptist, June 1945.

Chapter 17: Alfonso Gaspar Taqueban Makil

Brichoux, Felicia S. *Gaspar the Second King.* Grand Forks, North Dakota: Summer Institute of Linguistics, 1970.

Moody Bible Institute Academic Records, Gaspar Makil.

Hefley, James, and Marti Hefley. *By Their Blood: Christian Martyrs of the Twentieth Century.* Grand Rapids: Baker, 1996.

Nicholas, Gertrude. "Josephine Mikal, a Life Well-Lived, May 7, 1932–April 25, 2003." Wycliffe. http://www.wycliffe.org/africanamerican/ makilj.htm.

Chapter 18: Arthur Francis Tylee

"Arthur F. Tylee Dedicatory Memorial Service." Church Bulletin of The Pleasant Street Baptist Church, Worcester, Mass., March 7, 1937.

Hefley, James, and Marti Hefley. *By Their Blood: Christian Martyrs of the Twentieth Century.* Grand Rapids: Baker, 1998.

"Extract of a Letter Written by Rev. Arthur F. Tylee, Oct. 1930," *Inland South America,* March 1931.

Davis, Joseph A. "In Memoriam Arthur Francis Tylee, An Appreciation." *Inland South America,* May 1933.

Lake, Kenneth (field leader SAM, Brazil). March 2003. Interview by Marvin Newell.

McDowell, Albert. Personal letter, from Posadas, Argentina, February 7, 1931.

Moody Bible Institute Academic Records, Arthur Tylee.

Tylee, Ethel Canary. "A Letter from a Martyr's Home." *Moody Bible Institute Monthly,* June 1931.

Tylee, Arthur F. Excerpts of letters unpublished, no date.

Tylee, Mrs. Arthur. *The Challenge of Amazon's Indians.* Chicago: The Bible Institute Colportage Association, 1931.

Chapter 19: Mildred Pauline Kratz

Boston Sunday Post, "Jungle Witch Doctor's Jealous Rage Brings Martyrdom to Young Bay State Missionary and His Baby Daughter," February 22, 1931.

Hefley, James, and Marti Hefley. *By Their Blood: Christian Martyrs of the Twentieth Century.* Grand Rapids: Baker, 1998.

Kratz, Ronald. Personal letter to Reverend Kenneth MacKenzie, Westport, CT., November 28, 1930.

Moody Bible Institute Academic Records, Mildred Kratz.

Moody Bible Institute Martyrs. Unpublished document, no date.

Norwood, Edith B. "SAM's Hall of Fame: Ethel Canary, Tylee," no date.

Records of S.A.M., Billy Graham Archives, collection 204, Folders 1–7.

Tylee, Arthur. Prayer letter of September 1, 1930.

Chapter 20: Karl Bregenzer

Adams, Anna. *Moravian Missionaries in Nicaragua: The American Years, 1917–1974.* Ann Arbor, MI.: U.M.I., 1992.

Borhek, Mary Virginia. *Watchmen on the Walls.* Bethlehem, PA: The Society for Propagating the Gospel, 1949.

Hamilton, J. Taylor, and Kenneth G. Taylor. *History of the Moravian Church: The Renewed Unitas Fratrum.* Bethlehem, PA: Interprovincial Board of Christian Education Moravian Church in America, 1967.

Hamilton, Kenneth G. *Meet Nicaragua.* Bethlehem, PA: Comenius Press, 1939.

Moody Bible Institute Academic Records, Karl Bregenzer.

Chapter 21: Ancel Edwin Allen

"The Martyr Death of Ancel Allen." *Flight, Winging the Word to the Lost,* XIII, no. 4, May 1962.

Getz, Gene A. *MBI—The Story of Moody Bible Institute,* Chicago: Moody, 1986.

Hefley, James, and Marti Hefley. *By Their Blood: Christian Martyrs of the Twentieth Century.* 2nd ed. Grand Rapids: Baker, 1996.

Moody Bible Institute Academic Records, Ancel Edwin Allen.

Moody Monthly, November 1956, page 7.

Phone interview with Jeannette Allen, August, 2005.

Phone interview with Karen Begley, August 2005.

"Son Dies in Plane Crash." *The North Vernon Sun,* Tuesday, September 25, 1956.

Woodbridge, John D., ed. *Ambassadors for Christ.* Chicago: Moody, 1994.

Putting Martyrdom in Perspective

Bergman, Susan. *Martyrs.* San Francisco: Harper Collins, 1996.

Droge, Arthur J., and James D. Tabor. *A Noble Death.* San Francisco: Harper, 1992.

Emerson, Ralph Waldo. "Essays: Compensation." www.bartleby.com/5/105.html.

"The Martyr Death of Ancel Allen," *Flight, Winging the Word to the Lost,* XIII, no. 4, May 1962.

Hefley, James, and Marti Hefley. *By Their Blood: Christian Martyrs of the Twentieth Century.* Grand Rapids: Baker, 1996.

"Martyr Definition," adopted by executive cabinet of Moody Bible Institute, unpublished document, March 2001.

"Paoting Fu—Its Sad Memories." *China's Millions,* 1901.

Taylor, F. Howard. *These Forty Years: A Short History of the China Inland Mission.* Philadelphia: Pepper Publishing, 1903.

Tson, Josef. *Suffering, Martyrdom and Rewards in Heaven.* Lamham: University Press of America, Inc., 1997.

White, Karen L. "Overcoming Resistance through Martyrdom." *Reaching the Resistant: Barriers and Bridges for Missions.* Edited by J. Dudley Woodbury. Evangelical Missiological Society Series #6. Pasadena: William Carey Library, 1998.

A Biography from Moody Publishers:
D. L. Moody—A Life

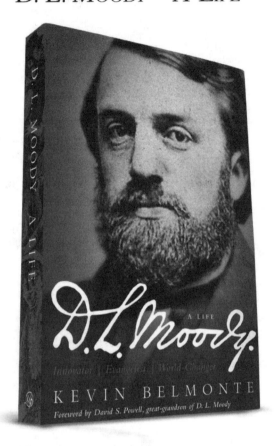

He burst on the fusty corridors of Victorian spirituality like a breath of fresh air, regaling one prime minister with his sense of humor and touching the lives of seven presidents.

Who was this man? A visionary educator and fundraiser, D. L. Moody was also a renowned evangelist in the nineteenth century. Long before radio and television, he brought the transformative message of the gospel before 100 million people on both sides of the Atlantic.

Drawing on the best, most recent scholarship, *D. L. Moody—A Life* chronicles the incredible journey of one of the great souls of history.

MOODY
Publishers™

From the Word to Life